INSIGHT GUIDES

İSTANBUL

smart guide

Contents

Highlights

▲ **Topkapı Palace** Soak up imperial splendour and get a glimpse of the magnificence of the Ottomans in their glory days.

▶ **Grand Bazaar** Give the locals a run for their money in this famed and ferociously busy bazaar.

◀ **Bosphorus Boat Cruise** Sightsee from the Bosphorus for the most romantic view of the city's ancient monuments.

▲ **İstiklal Caddesi** Stroll up and down this trendy thoroughfare in the 'new' part of the city.

▲ **Aya Sofya** Think yourself back to the Middle Ages before the glittering Byzantine mosaics of this glorious structure.

◀ **Sultanahmet Mosque** Soak up the atmosphere in this stupendous building crowned with cascading domes.

İstanbul

At the start of the 21st century İstanbul is on a roll. The one-time capital of the Eastern Roman, Byzantine and Ottoman Empires may have ceded that title to Ankara, but this is a city with an enthusiastic young population ensuring that exciting new shops, restaurants, bars and nightclubs are opening every day amid the extraordinary reminders of the past.

İstanbul Facts and Figures

Area: 5,343 sq km (2,063 sq miles)
Population: 12,915,158 (2009 census)
Population growth since 1950: 1,000 percent
Percentage of population under twenty: 32 percent
Projected population growth per hour (to 2025): 14
Number of mosques in İstanbul: 2,944 (2007)
Highest point: Çamlıca Hill (288 metres/945ft)
Length of city walls: 22km (14 miles)
Length of Bosphorus: 32km (20 miles)
Average width of Bosphorus: 2,100 metres (6,890ft)
Ships transiting Bosphorus annually: 50,000
Accidents involving ships passing along Bosphorus between 1988 and 2009: c.300
İstanbul – also known as: Asitane, Byzantium, Constantinople, Dersaadet, Islambol, Konstantiniyye, Stamboul

East Meets West

It may be a cliché but it's none the less true for all that. İstanbul is the only city in the world that quite literally straddles two continents, with one side of the Bosphorus strait in Europe and the other in Asia. Not surprisingly the city's culture exactly reflects that divide, being an intoxicating mix of Western and Middle Eastern culture. Sit down for a meal in one of the fashionable fusion restaurants, then end the evening in a *nargile* (waterpipe) café and you'll understand exactly why it is that İstanbul – and by extension Turkish – politics sometimes seem torn in two different directions at once.

Looking Back

When it comes to tourism İstanbul can hardly help but harp on its glorious past as the capital of three consecutive empires. The evidence of that glory is all around you especially if you choose to stay in Sultanahmet where the most splendid monuments – Topkapı Palace, Aya Sofya (Church of Holy Wisdom) and the Blue Mosque – are rarely more than a five-minute walk away. Even the most mundane café sometimes turns out to be housed inside a building dating back to the 16th century, and it's hard for any development to take place here since to dig down below the pavement is almost always to disturb the layered evidence of the past.

Looking Forward

But for all the importance of history to the tourist industry, modern İstanbul is really a city in a hurry, keen to move forward and more interested really in developing its transport infrastructure to cope with the burgeoning population and ever-increasing traffic than in taking the necessary time to restore every last reminder of

Below: the Fatih Camii is one of İstanbul's many fine mosques.

Above: the stunning night view of Sultanahmet from across the Golden Horn.

Byzantium at the slow pace that might be ideal. For the last few years life in Yenikapı and Üsküdar has been much disrupted by work on the Marmaray, a huge project to build a tunnel beneath the Bosphorus and connect it to the suburban train services on either side of it. Due to be completed in 2011, it has been delayed by discovery of the medieval port at Yenikapı during excavations, but should eventually make a big difference to ease of movement around the city. More controversially, the go-ahead has now been given to build a third bridge across the Bosphorus, which environmentalists fear will see the loss of yet more green space.

Wider and Wider Still

Hard though it may be to believe it now, at the start of the 20th century İstanbul was home to barely one million people. Today new residents are still trickling in and the city is struggling to cope with a population estimated at anything between 12 and 16 million depending on where you start and stop counting. Much of this immigration is attributable to the troubles that have plagued the southeast of Turkey since the mid-1980s and that drove many to leave their homes in search of a better life here. Many originally settled in *gecekondus*, properties that were literally thrown up overnight with no thought for aesthetics. Slowly the government is rehousing people in high-rise blocks on the outskirts of town which is pushing ever further outwards into Thrace (Europe) and Anatolia (Asia). Most visitors barely glimpse these rather depressing Soviet-style developments although they form a big part of modern İstanbul reality.

All Things to All People

It may be a giant, densely built-up megacity but Greater İstanbul also encompasses beaches at Şile and Kilyos, woodland in the Belgrade Forest and islands in the Sea of Marmara. There are world-class restaurants here, and shopping malls to give the US a run for its money. Above all, there is the Bosphorus, the wonderful waterway that makes the perfect escape whenever the pressure of heat and traffic threatens to get to you. No visit to İstanbul is complete without taking at least one trip on it even if only from one side of it to the other.

5

Sultanahmet and Kumkapı

Sultanahmet is the name generally used to describe the heart of İstanbul. It was here that the Byzantines made their capital and, in turn, so did the Ottomans, which means that you can hardly take a step without stumbling over reminders of the past. All the main monuments are here – Topkapı Palace, the Blue Mosque and Aya Sofya – as well as two of the most important museums, the İstanbul Archaeology Museum and the Museum of Turkish and Islamic Arts. There are many hotels and restaurants to cater for visitors, though you may want to wander downhill to Kumkapı where you can eat fish a stone's throw from the Sea of Marmara.

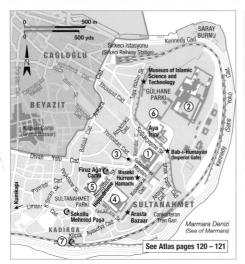

Above: flowers carpet Gülhane Park.

SULTANAHMET SQUARE

The heart of İstanbul is Sultanahmet Square which is dominated by the vast domed pile of **Aya Sofya** ①, the church where many of the Byzantine emperors were crowned and then the mosque where several of the sultans were buried. Facing it across the square is the most lavish of all hamams (Turkish baths), built for Haseki Hürrem Sultan, the wife of Süleyman the Magnificent. Follow the crowds

round the corner to find **Topkapı Palace** ② that was home to the sultans until the mid-19th century. It's likely to be marginally less busy below ground in the **Basilica Cistern** ③, an eerily atmospheric ancient reservoir.

SEE ALSO MONUMENTS, P.72; MOSQUES, SYNAGOGUES AND CHURCHES, P.78; PALACES, P.92

HIPPODROME

It's easy to stroll around the Hippodrome, which looks rather like an oblong park,

without realising that this was once the scene of Byzantine chariot races. Beside it, however, no one overlooks the graceful, six-minareted **Blue Mosque** ④, known to the locals as Sultanahmet Camii and almost 1,000 years younger than Aya Sofya which it faces across another small park. Also on the Hippodrome is the **Turkish and Islamic Arts Museum** ⑤, housed in what was once a nobleman's palace.

SEE ALSO MOSQUES, SYNAGOGUES AND CHURCHES, P.79; MUSEUMS AND GALLERIES, P.85

GÜLHANE PARK

If you want to see where local people go to relax you could do worse than

fare lined with shops and restaurants, amongst which historic monuments lurk almost apologetically. Look out for the little **Firuz Ağa Camii**, one of the city's oldest mosques, and for the graveyard containing the tombs of Sultans Mahmud II, Abdülaziz and Abdülhamid II.

KÜÇÜK AYA SOFYA

If you head downhill from behind the Arasta Bazaar you will come eventually to **Küçük Aya Sofya (Little Aya Sofya)** ⑦, a church-mosque that is older even than Aya Sofya. The *medrese* surrounding the courtyard hosts a small café, and the surrounding streets are turning into an arty little enclave with craft workshops.

SEE ALSO MOSQUES, SYNAGOGUES AND CHURCHES, P.78

KADIRGA AND KUMKAPI

Until recently Küçük Aya Sofya was as far as tourism went. Now, however, hotels are opening up in Kadırga, site of the old Byzantine port, where they rub shoulders with newly restored wooden houses. Kumkapı has long been a favourite place to eat fish. The fishing fleet still sets sail from here every day so the fish is guaranteed to be fresh.

SEEE ALSO RESTAURANTS, P.98

> The great Ottoman architect Sinan (c.1490-1588) has 42 mosques in İstanbul to his name. The nearest to Sultanahmet is the Sokollu Mehmed Paşa Mosque which straddles the hillside above Kadırga.

> The pretty little Arasta Bazaar behind the Blue Mosque was originally built to provide funds for its upkeep. Today it houses some of the city's more exclusive and original shops.

stroll through Gülhane Park on a summer Sunday when what was once part of the exclusive grounds of the Topkapı Palace becomes crowded. When people-watching gets too much you can always explore the **Museum of History of Islamic Science and Technology** against the park walls.

A path leads from the park to the **İstanbul Archaeology Museum** ⑥, stuffed like the British Museum with the pickings of imperialism, in this case of the Ottoman Empire.

SEE ALSO MUSEUMS AND GALLERIES, P.85; PARKS, GARDENS AND BEACHES, P.96

DİVAN YOLU

Everyone eventually finds their way to Divan Yolu, whether they are heading for the Grand Bazaar or just hopping on the tram to get about the city. Once this was the route walked by the sultans' viziers when they were heading to the *Divan* (Council Chamber) in Topkapı Palace to discuss imperial business. Today it's a busy thorough-

Below: the Sokollu Mehmed Paşa Mosque.

Beyazıt and Fatih

A short walk west of Sultanahmet, Beyazıt is home to the famous Grand Bazaar, a mini-city of some 4,000 shops. On the way to the Bazaar you'll pass the battered Çemberlitaş, one of the last reminders of Constantine the Great, the emperor who gave the city its old name, Constantinople. Behind the Bazaar stand two magnificent works of Sinan, the Süleymaniye and Şehzade mosques, both close to the much older Aqueduct of Valens. As you head further east into Fatih tourism starts to drop away. It picks up again around the Chora Church, whose mosaics and frescoes provide some of the most vivid echoes of Byzantium.

See Atlas pages 114, 119, 120

Like Rome, Byzantium was built on seven hills, most of them topped with a mosque or palace.

have a great time trying to bargain with the shop-keepers. The best way to approach the Bazaar is via the courtyard of the **Nuruosmaniye Mosque** which leads to the grandest of the entrances.

The square beside the Bazaar is home to the huge and peaceful **Beyazıt Mosque,** as well as to İstanbul University, the oldest in the city.

When you have finished shopping the **Çorlulu Ali Paşa Medresesi,** a historic *nargile* (waterpipe) café, is a perfect place to end the day.

SEE ALSO BARS AND CAFÉS, P.30; MOSQUES, SYNAGOGUES AND CHURCHES, P.79; BAZAARS AND SHOPPING, P.35

Above: exploring the large Fatih Mosque.

although battered by fate since then, hence the iron hoops that hold it together. Just across the road **Çemberlitaş Hamam** is a beautiful work of Sinan and one of the best places in town to acquire the Turkish bathing habit.
SEE ALSO HAMAMS AND SPAS, P.56

GRAND BAZAAR (KAPALI ÇARŞI)

Also known as the Covered Bazaar (Kapalı Çarşı in Turkish), the **Grand Bazaar** ① is not a place for the faint-hearted. Critics have been complaining about the touts since at least the mid-19th century, but on a good day you'll

ÇEMBERLİTAŞ

Once the Forum of Constantine, today's Çemberlitaş Square is an architectural mess but does boast the **Çemberlitaş Column** ②, erected during the lifetime of Constantine the Great

SÜLEYMANİYE

On the summit of old İstanbul's third hill stands the **Süleymaniye Mosque** ③, said to be the greatest of all Sinan's works in the city and recently completely restored. It stands at the centre of a vast mosque complex including a caravanserai, soup kitchen and assorted

and slightly later version of the Çemberlitaş Column. While in Fatih you might also want to seek out the **Fethiye Mosque-Museum**, a wonderful, mosaic-filled Byzantine church that was turned into a mosque and is now a museum that deserves to be much better known.

SEE ALSO MONUMENTS, P.74; MOSQUES, SYNAGOGUES AND CHURCHES, P.79

EDİRNEKAPI

Edirnekapı takes its name from the gate in the city walls through which ran the road to Edirne in Thrace. The main reason to venture out this far is to visit the glorious mosaic and fresco-filled **Chora Church (Kariye Museum)** ⑦, a small Byzantine church that was given a makeover during the Byzantine renaissance of the 13th century. While here you might also want to take a look at the **Mihrimah Sultan Mosque,** designed by Sinan to crown the city's sixth hill.

SEE ALSO MOSQUES, SYNAGOGUES AND CHURCHES, P.82

> Every Wednesday a huge market fills the streets of Çarşamba, the hyper-conservative area immediately behind the Fatih Mosque.

medreses (seminaries) that illustrate the crucial role mosques played in Ottoman social life. Nearby, the **Şehzade Mosque** ④ is older than the Süleymaniye and many consider it just as beautiful.

From beside the Süleymaniye you can trace the route of the **Aqueduct of Valens** ⑤, a crucial link in the system that used to supply the city with water.

SEE ALSO MONUMENTS, P.74; MOSQUES, SYNAGOGUES AND CHURCHES, P.80

FATİH

One of old İstanbul's more conservative neighbourhoods, Fatih lives for the fortress-like **Fatih Mosque** ⑥, built for Sultan Mehmed II (el-Fatih, 'the Conqueror'), the man who seized Constantinople for the Turks in 1453. Within walking distance is the **Sultan Selim Mosque,** designed by Sinan for Selim I and sited to offer a sweeping view over the Golden Horn.

Also nearby is the **Kıztaşı,** a lesser-known

Below: traffic pours through the Aqueduct of Valens.

Eminönü and the Golden Horn

Eminönü is the waterfront of old İstanbul where ferries leave for Kadıköy, Üsküdar and the Bosphorus. Its landmarks are unmissable, the New Mosque, the Spice Market and the Galata Bridge – although the terminal for ferries along the Golden Horn keeps a low profile. Also look out for the huge old Fener Boys High School, the cast-iron church of St Stephen, the sprawling cemetery of Eyüp, and the old Galata Bridge now rebuilt to serve as a footbridge between Eyüp and Sütlüce.

See Atlas pages 120 – 121

EMİNÖNÜ

Most people pause in Eminönü only to buy a jeton for the ferry or to eat a fish sandwich from one of the floating kitchens moored beside the Galata Bridge. On the inland side of the hectic coastal highway the **New Mosque (Yeni Camii)** ① dates back to 1660. Funds to maintain it were generated from sales of herbs and spices in the little **Spice Market** ② beside it. Nowadays the surrounding streets are at least as interesting as those inside the Spice Market. Even more interesting are the narrow streets of nearby **Tahtakale**, where the locals shop for everyday items in the shadow of the **Rüstem Paşa Mosque** ③, a popular work of Sinan that sits on a stone platform above the shops.
SEE ALSO BAZAARS AND SHOPPING, P.37; MOSQUES, SYNAGOGUES AND CHURCHES, P.80

> Poke about in **Tahtakale** and you will find several crumbling hans, medieval trading centres that provided rooms and stabling for passing traders as well. The most atmospheric huddle around the base of the Rüstem Paşa Mosque.

FENER

Once home to many wealthy Greeks who continued to flourish under the Ottomans, Fener is now a cramped, crowded quarter whose monuments often go unnoticed. For Greek Orthodox Christians, however, the **Greek Patriarchate** ④ continues to be their equivalent of the Vatican which means particularly crowded services at Easter. More conspicuous is the waterside **Church of St Stephen of the Bulgars**, a rare example of a completely cast-iron church. Dominating the skyline is the red-brick **Fener Greek Boys High School,** frequently mistaken for the Patriarchate.
SEE ALSO MOSQUES, SYNAGOGUES AND CHURCHES, P.83

BALAT

Fener merges seamlessly with equally delapidated Balat, once home to much of İstanbul's Jewish population. Their finest reminder is the lovely **Ahrida Syna-**

Below: at the Spice Market in Eminönü.

Left: at the entrance to the welcoming New Mosque.

SEE ALSO BARS AND CAFÉS, P.29; MOSQUES, SYNAGOGUES AND CHURCHES, P.80; WALKS AND VIEWS, P.110

SÜTLÜCE

Until recently an industrial wasteland, Sütlüce and the area immediately to the north of it has seen a lot of investment to make it more attractive and is now home to **Santralİstanbul,** a cutting-edge art gallery housed, like London's Tate Modern, in a decommissioned power station. Nearby **Miniatürk** is a rare attraction designed with children in mind.
SEE ALSO CHILDREN, P.40; MUSEUMS AND GALLERIES, P.86

HASKÖY

Once the site of a shipyard, Hasköy is now home to the **Rahmi M. Koç Museum** ⑦, a lively historical museum with inviting restaurants in the grounds.
SEE ALSO CHILDREN, P.40

Galata Bridge links Eminönü with equally busy Karaköy. No matter what the time of day its topside is bound to be lined with fishermen while its underside is thick with fish restaurants.

---

gogue, although arrangements for visiting it are singularly off-putting. Instead you can enjoy strolling the back streets with their crumbling rowhouses or browsing in the small local market.
SEE ALSO MOSQUES, SYNAGOGUES AND CHURCHES, P.82

AYVANSARAY

At Ayvansaray the **Theodosian Walls** that protected the city's landward side met the less dramatic sea walls. If you follow the walls inland you will come to the remains of the **Tekfur Palace** ⑤, possibly

part of the Blachernae Palace which replaced Topkapı in the late-13th century. It stood close to a sacred spring now inside the **Blachernae Church.**
SEE ALSO MONUMENTS, P.77

EYÜP

The holiest place in İstanbul, the **Eyüp Sultan Mosque** ⑥ was where newly crowned sultans went to be given the Sword of Osman, the first sultan of the Ottoman dynasty. Dignitaries jostled each other for the right to be buried nearby and the mosque, which contains the shrine of a companion of the Prophet Mohammed, is ringed with elaborate and beautiful funerary complexes. From the famous **Pierre Loti Café** there is a sweeping view of the Golden Horn.

See Atlas pages 114 – 115

Karaköy, Tophane and Beşiktaş

In Ottoman times, the area to the north of what is now the Galata Bridge was home to foreign communities. Karaköy is a port area, once part of the virtually independent Genoese trading colony and later a centre for banking. The monuments get grander at Tophane, home to the old Ottoman arsenal. This segues into Dolmabahçe where the later sultans made their palace, and then into Beşiktaş, a crowded residential area whose narrow shopping streets contrast with the grandeur of the minor palaces that line the Bosphorus.

KARAKÖY

Most people rush through Karaköy on the tram or linger only long enough to catch a ferry to Kadıköy or Haydarpaşa Station. At the end of the street beside the entrance to the Tünel funicular railway,

Below: a detail on the Tophane Fountain.

however, it's worth visiting the old Zülfaris Synagogue which now houses a small **Jewish Museum** ①. Another quirky monument is the **Yeraltı (Underground) Mosque** near the large Turkish Maritime Lines building which contains the graves of two sixth-century warriors. A chain attached to a tower on the same site was once used to close the Golden Horn to foreign shipping.

Stroll along **Voyvoda (Bankalar) Caddesi** to admire the Victorian-style grandeur of the buildings erected here to house 19th-century banks. Most are now headquartered in thoroughly modern Maslak.
SEE ALSO MUSEUMS AND GALLERIES, P.84

TOPHANE

Dominated by the multi-domed arsenal building

(tophane) from which it took its name, Tophane is home to a late work of Sinan, the **Kılıç Ali Paşa Mosque** ②, whose hamam should soon be returning to life after restoration. The focal point of a small green is the elaborate 18th-century **Tophane Fountain**, and, behind it, a row of lively *nargile* (waterpipe) cafés. The **Nüsretiye Mosque** was built in 1826 to commemorate Sultan Mahmud II's victory over the rebellious Janissary troops. One of the warehouses behind it has been restored to house the **İstanbul Modern** ③, a wonderful, light-filled gallery that has breathed new life into the İstanbul art scene since 2005.
SEE ALSO BARS AND CAFÉS, P.30; MOSQUES, SYNAGOGUES AND CHURCHES, P.80; MUSEUMS AND GALLERIES, P.86

Left: in the stately Dolmabahçe Palace.

Square with, to one side, the **Naval Museum** ⑤, home to a fine collection of the gondola-like caiques used to ferry the sultans about the Bosphorus.

At one time many of the minor aristocracy had palaces on the waterfront here. One now houses the **Four Seasons İstanbul at the Bosphorus** hotel, while another has been reconstructed to house the very luxurious **Çırağan Palace Kempinski Hotel** ⑥, with a superb infinity swimming pool. Across the road is **Yıldız Park** ⑦ a green lung for the city which slithers down the hillside. Inside the park is a complex of buildings that made up the palace of the paranoid sultan Abdülhamid II, as well as a pair of small museums and a number of delightful cafés.

Hidden in the back streets of Beşiktaş is **Ihlamur Kasrı**, where two pavilions provide an attractive photographic backdrop for newly-married couples emerging from the registry office across the road.

SEE ALSO HOTELS, P.63; MUSEUMS AND GALLERIES, P.86; PALACES, P.95

Ten years ago the *nargile* (waterpipe) had all but died a death in Turkey. Visit the row of cafés at Tophane to marvel at its recovery – and at the way it has survived premature fears that the smoking ban of 2009 would kill it off again.

SEE ALSO MOSQUES, SYNAGOGUES AND CHURCHES, P.81; PALACES, P.93; SPORT, P.104

DOLMABAHÇE

Completed on reclaimed land in 1856, the ornate **Dolmabahçe Palace** ④ was home to most of the later sultans who forsook Topkapı in a forlorn endeavour to pull the Ottoman Empire into line with the modern world. Beside it stands the frequently overlooked but airy and attractive **Dolmabahçe Mosque,** while across the road stands the **BJK İnönü Stadium,** a monument to Turkey's love affair with its football teams, in this case Beşiktaş, the 'Black Eagles'.

BEŞIKTAŞ

Beşiktaş is a somewhat amorphous, mainly residential area with lively shopping streets interspersed with cheap eateries aimed at the large student population. The waterfront is dominated by Barbaros

Below: the historical ferry pier in Beşiktaş.

Kabataş is a major transport interchange, the terminus of the tramway from Sultanahmet where it connects with the modern funicular railway up to Taksim Square. Ferries from Kabataş run out to the Princes' Islands, while buses ply the Bosphorus coast road to Ortaköy and points beyond.

13

Beyoğlu

In the 19th century Beyoğlu was the part of town favoured by İstanbul's foreign communities. Today its hectic streets are some of the most vibrant in all the city – this is by far the best place to come to take the pulse of young, modern Turkey, with restaurants, bars, shops and clubs opening and closing with astonishing rapidity. The focal point of the action is İstiklal Caddesi, a lengthy pedestrianised street with an old tram running along it. Recently the most lively area has migrated south from around Taksim Square to Galata and Asmalımescit, packed with a crush of pavement tables at weekends. A few hours here make the perfect antidote to an excess of historic sightseeing.

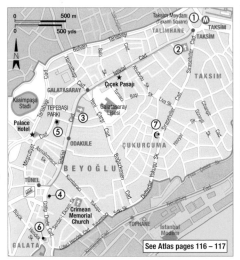

See Atlas pages 116 – 117

Above: the streets off İstiklal Caddesi are a good place to come for eating and drinking.

TAKSİM SQUARE

The Turkish answer to Trafalgar Square or Times Square is Taksim Meydanı, partly an unsightly traffic intersection, partly a symbolic reminder of the Turkish War of Independence (1919-22) that led to the founding of the contemporary state. This historic aspect of Taksim is summed up by the **Republic Monument** ① that stands in front of what was once the outside wall of one of the city's stone reservoirs;

water from it was fed into the dainty octagonal building (the *taksim*) nearby for distribution. Looming over one corner of the square is the enormous church of **Aygia Triada** ②, a reminder of the city's once large Greek population.

SEE ALSO MONUMENTS, P.77; MOSQUES, SYNAGOGUES AND CHURCHES, P.83

İSTİKLAL CADDESİ

There's nowhere better in Turkey, let alone İstanbul, to get a feel for what the

modern country is about than this ever-busy, ever-crowded pedestrianised thoroughfare that feels rather like a canyon lined with grand 19th-century mansions and apartment blocks interspersed with more low-profile churches. The **nostalgic tram** is always good for a ride, especially if you've done a lot of sightseeing although it takes its time about the journey from one end of the street to the other. Specific sites to

Left: flying the flag in Taksim Square.

Off the west side of Taksim Square is Talimhane, a newly fashionable and pedestrianised zone that is full of hotels. It is one of the few districts in the city that has a wide range of restaurants that offer non-Turkish dishes.

trading colony, Galata is dominated by the unmissable **Galata Tower** ⑥, the building with the witch's-hat roof that dominates the Beyoğlu skyline. The smaller, lumpier tower nearby was once the British Hospital and stood near a private British jail, now home to a Georgian restaurant.
SEE ALSO MONUMENTS, P.76

look out for include **Çiçek Pasajı (Flower Passage)** and the crowded streets of Nevizade behind it where people come to tuck into mezes and fish washed down with plenty of rakı; and **St Anthony's Cathedral** ③, the largest and most prominent of the old Christian places of worship.
SEE ALSO MOSQUES, SYNGOGUES AND CHURCHES, P.83; RESTAURANTS, P.102

TÜNEL AND ASMALIMESCİT
The **Tünel** is a handy one-stop funicular linking Kar-

If you're interested in the whirling dervishes then the **Galata Mevlevihanesi** ④ is one of the most atmospheric places to watch an authentic *sema* (ritual performance) taking place. Dates and times vary but are listed on a board outside.

aköy to İstiklal Caddesi that brings you out within a short walk of trendy **Asmalımescit** which is full of places to eat and drink. It's also within walking distance of the state-of-the-art **Pera Museum** ⑤ which hosts excellent visiting art exhibitions as well as a small permanent collection.
Nearby is the famous **Pera Palace Hotel** where Agatha Christie dreamt up her famous novel, *Murder on the Orient Express*. The **Crimean Memorial Church** is an unexpected little reminder of England hiding behind a high wall in what is an increasingly fashionable corner of town.
SEE ALSO HOTELS, P.65; MUSEUMS AND GALLERIES, P.86

GALATA
Once home to a large self-governing Genoese

SIRASELVİLER CADDESİ
Running off Taksim square at an oblique angle is this narrow and congested street which is home to some very fashionable restaurants and hotels. Locals congregate to sip tea in the shade of a tree in front of the small and architecturally undistinguished **Firuz Ağa Mosque** ⑦.

ÇUKURCUMA
If you are interested in buying, or browsing for, antiques then you should definitely head for this rapidly gentrifying neighbourhood squeezed in between İstiklal and Sıraselviler caddesis. Old marble fountains, reconditioned chairs, embroidered towels and pillowcases are all here, albeit at prices you may not always want to pay.

15

Nişantaşı, Teşvikiye and Maçka

I f İstiklal Caddesi is the place to see young Turkey, Nişantaşı is the place to encounter a rather more sedate and monied crowd. Its an old part of the city which means that the streets are often narrow and rather crowded, but if you're after high-end labels this is the place to do your shopping. Nişantaşı merges seamlessly into Teşvikiye and Maçka where there are several upmarket hotels. The one real draw for sightseers is the Military (Askeri) Museum, technically in the neighbouring district of Harbiye.

ABDİ İPEKÇİ CADDESİ

Running all the way from Valikonağı Caddesi to Maçka Caddesi, Abdi İpekçi Caddesi is one of İstanbul's foremost shopping streets especially when it comes to designer labels. Pay this street a visit if you are look-ing for Cartier, Prada and **Alexander McQueen** but also to see and be seen in expensive restaurants such as the popular **Beyman Brasserie**.
SEE ALSO FASHION, P.47; RESTAURANTS, P.103

VALİKONAĞI CADDESİ

Valikonağı Caddesi is one the gateways into Nişantaşı from busy Halaskargazi Caddesi, the

Above: the cool and shady Maçka Park.

long road that wends its way from Taksim Square to Şişli. For non-shoppers the first port of call should be the **Military (Askeri) Museum** ①, once a mili-tary academy attended by

It's hard to imagine now that this was once an imperial hunting ground but in the courtyard of the Teşvikiye Mosque stand several of the arrow stones (*nişan taşı*) after which Nişantaşı was named – they marked the maximum distance a sultan had managed to fire his bow that day. There's another at the road junction where Valikonağı Caddesi crosses Teşvikiye Caddesi.

Atatürk, the founder of the Turkish Republic, and the venue now for lively and loud performances by the Ottoman Mehter Band. A little further up the road on the left a mansion with a brightly tiled façade, the **Vedat Tek Konağı** ②, was once home to a leading exponent of a style of architecture called First National that was popular in the early 20th century.
SEE ALSO ARCHITECTURE, P.27; MUSEUMS AND GALLERIES, P.87

TEŞVİKİYE CADDESİ

Running parallel with Abdi İpekçi Caddesi, Teşvikiye Caddesi is a little more down to earth as a place to shop with branches of international chain stores

Below: rockets at Nişantaşı's Military Museum.

Left: Nişantaşı is the place for designer shopping.

Demokrasi parks extend on either side of a valley, both great places to take a breather from shopping, perhaps with a cool drink at one of the tea gardens lining their edges. A rarely noticed cable car runs from in front of the **Maçka Barracks** ⑦ to Taksim, offering a quick way to get back to the centre.

HALASKARGAZİ CADDESI

The main road that runs from Taksim Square to Şişli is always busy, and you have to look hard to notice the occasional lovely 19th-century mansion block amid the concrete high-rises. One powder-pink wooden house is worth a quick look. Since Atatürk lived in it briefly with his mother and sister it has been turned into a small museum in his memory, the only one in İstanbul.

such as Zara, Benetton and Mothercare. It's home, too, to the **City's Shopping Mall** ③, one of İstanbul's more centrally located undercover shopping centres, as well as to a branch of the Sütte delicatessen chain. For sightseers the main point of interest will be **Teşvikiye Mosque** ④, a society mosque where the funerals of celebrities such as that of Ahmet Ertegün, founder of Atlantic Records, sometimes take place. Nearby, The House Café is housed inside an old *sebil* ⑤, one of the street-corner fountains from which cold drinks used to be dispensed to passers-by in Ottoman times. Two very smart hotels, the **Sofa** and the **Park Hyatt** ⑥, can also be found here.

SEE ALSO BAZAARS AND SHOPPING, P.36; HOTELS, P.66; MONUMENTS, P.74; MOSQUES, SYNAGOGUES AND CHURCHES, P.81

MAÇKA AND DEMOKRASİ PARKS

Just off Abdi İpekçi Caddesi the Maçka and

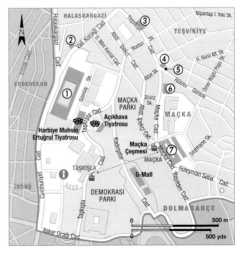

The Bosphorus

If there is one feature that marks İstanbul out from comparable historic cities it is probably the Bosphorus, the extraordinary strait that slices through the city as it makes its way from the Black Sea to the Sea of Marmara, dividing it into separate European and Asian parts. Of great strategic importance, the Bosphorus has been the focus of many conflicts over the centuries. Today all is peaceful but busy with ships in all shapes and sizes plying up and down and from side to side. Even on the shortest visit you should certainly take to the water at least once to get a real feel for life in İstanbul.

Above: an Arnavutköy house.

EUROPEAN SHORE

The European shore of the Bosphorus runs from Karaköy to Rumeli Feneri.

ORTAKÖY

Ortaköy is one of İstanbul's most fashionable nightclub areas and the coast road here is congested. Come here to dine or browse at a crafts market on Sundays.

SEE ALSO BAZAARS AND SHOPPING, P.36

KURUÇEŞME AND ARNAVUTKÖY

The Ortaköy action continues in Kuruçeşme where a small island is completely devoted to restaurants and nightlife. At Arnavutköy there are a string of attractive wooden houses lining the shore.

SEE ALSO ARCHITECTURE, P.27; NIGHTLIFE, P.91

BEBEK AND RUMELİ HISARI

Bebek is very trendy and the main road is full of restaurants and boutiques. The most conspicuous monument is the huge Art Nouveau building on the waterside that used to house the **Egyptian Consulate** ①. There

is a short walk north to Rumeli Hisarı. Named after the huge castle built here by Mehmed II prior to the siege of Constaninople, this suburb is still dominated by the restored ruins of the **castle** ②, but also some pleasant cafés.

SEE ALSO MONUMENTS, P.77; WALKS AND VIEWS, P.111

EMİRGAN

The Emirgan Woods are one of the best places to visit in April when the annual Tulip Festival is in full swing. At other times of year the main draw is the **Sakıp Sabancı Museum** ③, whose permanent collection is often supplemented with blockbuster travelling shows.

SEE ALSO MUSEUMS AND GALLERIES, P.87; PARKS, GARDENS AND BEACHES, P.96

BÜYÜKDERE

The 'Big Valley' rather a long way up the Bosphorus but it's home to the **Sadberk Hanım Museum** ④, which contains good collections of archaeology and ethnography.

SEE ALSO MUSEUMS AND GALLERIES, P.87

Two bridges – the Bosphorus and the Fatih Sultan Mehmet – already cross the Bosphorus. A third is to run from Garipçe in Europe to Poyrazköy in Asia.

SEE ALSO MONUMENTS, P.77; PALACES, P.95

ÇUBUKLU

The **Khedive's Villa** ⑦ is a partly Art Nouveau mansion with a soaring tower that can be seen from the grounds of the Sakıp Sabancı Museum. It was built for a 19th-century governor (*khedive*) of Egypt, hence its name. Come in April for the tulips.

ANADOLU KAVAĞI

Last stop on the İDO Bosphorus cruises is Anadolu Kavağı where people come to eat fish. The ferry stops long enough for most people to climb the hill to the ruins of Yoros Castle where there is a fine view along the Bosphorus and out to the Black Sea.

SEE ALSO BOAT TRIPS, P.38

The Bosphorus ('cow crossing' in Greek) takes its name from the Ancient Greek myth about Io, a girl seduced by Zeus, then turned into a cow to escape the wrath of his wife Hera. The strait is also associated with stories of Jason and the Argonauts as they made their way to Colchis in search of the Golden Fleece.

ASIAN SHORE

The Asian shore of the Bosphorus runs from Kadıköy to Anadolu Feneri.

BEYLERBEYİ

It is well worth crossing the Bosphorus and heading north from Üsküdar to visit the **Beylerbeyi Palace** ⑤, the summer palace built for Sultan Abdülaziz by members of the prolific Balyan architects. There is also a pleasing array of coffee shops and small fish restaurants spread out around the ferry terminal.

SEE ALSO PALACES, P.94

KANDİLLİ AND ANADOLU HİSARI

At Kandilli the **Göksu Deresi (river)** flows into the Bosphorus. Once known as 'the Sweet Waters of Asia', this used to be a popular pleasure ground and is recovering some of its erstwhile popularity after a recent clean-up campaign. Also here is the **Küçüksu Kasrı** ⑥, a 19th-century stone hunting lodge that, while ornate in style, is restrained compared to the Dolmabahçe Palace. The **castle** from which Anadolu Hisarı (Anatolian Castle) takes its name is slightly older than the one at Rumeli Hisarı but in much worse shape since a road was carved through its middle.

Below: at the Emirgan Woods Tulip Festival.

Kadıköy and Üsküdar

Easily accessible by ferry from Eminönü, Kadıköy and adjoining Üsküdar could hardly be more different. Kadıköy is a lively residential neighbourhood with good, cheap shops and plenty of nightlife. Üsküdar, on the other hand, has a reputation for conservatism, and houses a preponderance of historic mosques in place of bars. While in Kadıköy use the old-fashioned tram to visit the restaurants in Moda or go up to Fenerbahçe to watch a football match. You might also take a walk along Bağdat Caddesi (Baghdad Street), a wide shopping street. In between Kadıköy and Üsküdar is Haydarpaşa, from where trains to Anatolia start.

Above: on lively 'Bar Street' in Kadıköy.

Non-sports fans might like to take a turn round **Fenerbahçe Park,** a pretty oasis on a peninsula jutting out into the Sea of Marmara that is especially lovely in spring. SEE ALSO SPORT, P.104

KADIKÖY

Kadıköy is the Beşiktaş of Asian İstanbul with a network of tiny shopping streets selling the freshest produce at the best prices. Tucked in amid the shops are 19th-century churches that recall lost Greek and Armenian residents. **Bahariye Caddesi** ① is to Kadıköy what İstiklal Caddesi is to Beyoğlu; if you get the chance, catch a performance in the lavishly deco-rated **Sürreya Opera House** which started life as a cinema. **Kadife Sokak (Bar Street)** is the centre of the lively local nightlife scene, set in a series of restored wooden houses. SEE ALSO NIGHTLIFE, P.91

FENERBAHÇE

The name Fenerbahçe is synonymous with the much-loved football team (the 'Yellow Canaries') whose **stadium** ② is here.

BAĞDAT CADDESİ

Asian İstanbul's main shopping street will not strike most foreign visitors as much to look at but does feature all the big names in international retailing as well as a branch of the home-grown luxury department store Vakko. Running parallel with it, the Sahil Yolu (Shore Road) offers pleasant cafés and restaurants

Just south of Kadıköy **Moda** is worth visiting if only to have a light meal in the delightful decommissioned **Ferry Terminal 1**, now a restaurant (no alcohol) connected to the mainland by a causeway.

Just offshore is the **Maiden's Tower** ⑦, which has generated a succession of fantastic stories; you can pop across by boat to pay a visit although it is just as interesting from a distance.

Inland and uphill from Üsküdar are the twin beauty spots known as **Büyük (Big) and Küçük (Little) Çamlıca.** Büyük Çamlıca is the better known of the two and certainly has great views out to sea although its setting has been marred by the arrival of telephone and radio masts. Less well known Küçük Çamlıca is hillier and more secretive but with similarly great sea views and none of the off-putting masts.

SEE ALSO MOSQUES, SYNAGOGUES AND CHURCHES, P.81; WALKS AND VIEWS, P.111

The **Marmaray** project will eventually link Üsküdar to Yenikapı on the European side of the city via a tunnel under the sea. The suburban train services operating out of Haydarpaşa and Sirkeci stations will then be upgraded to provide one continuous route in an attempt to ease some of the city's notorious traffic congestion.

as well as fine places to take a walk with the locals on a summer evening.

SEE ALSO BAZAARS AND SHOPPING, P.35

HAYDARPAŞA

The huge **station** ③ that has seen passengers setting off towards Anatolia for more than a century looks likely to be decommissioned as soon as the Marmaray project is completed. Behind it stands the huge **Selimiye Bar-**racks, out of bounds to visitors but for the small **Florence Nightingale Museum.**

Nearby, too, is the sprawling **Karacaahmet Cemetery,** one of the city's largest, with, in one corner, the new and ultra-modern **Şakirin Mosque.**

SEE ALSO MOSQUES, SYNAGOGUES AND CHURCHES, P.82

ÜSKÜDAR

As soon as you step off the ferry at Üsküdar you'll see the large and impressive **İskele (Harbour) Mosque** ④, designed by Sinan and the first of several works by the architect to grace this suburb. Later in date but charming is the nearby **Yeni Valide Mosque** ⑤, although you'll need to be more determined to track down Sinan's **Atik Valide Mosque** ⑥, on the top of a hill some way inland.

Below: take a boat trip to visit Maiden's Tower.

Greater İstanbul

Modern İstanbul is one of the world's great metropolises, spreading ever wider on both sides of the Bosphorus into Europe (Thrace) and Asia (Anatolia). No one knows exactly how many people live in the suburbs but the city's population is estimated at anything between 12 and 16 million. Although visitors often confine their attentions to Sultanahmet and Beyoğlu some of the things to see and do actually lie some way away from the historic core. Public transport is improving all the time, but you'll find it time-consuming to reach some of the more remote sights. On the other hand you may well have them to yourself and the locals.

conquered by the Ottomans and subsequently renamed İstanbul.

SEE ALSO MONUMENTS, P.77; MUSEUMS AND GALLERIES, P.87

PRINCES' ISLANDS

At the height of summer İstanbul can be a hot and oppressive place, so it's good to know that you can join the locals in escaping by ferry to this small group of islands in the Sea of Marmara. Even better is that they are virtually traffic-free; people get around on foot, by bike or in horse-drawn carriages. Largest and most interesting of the islands is **Büyükada (Big Island),** where a rocky path leads up to **St George's Monastery** ③ and a panoramic view of İstanbul. There's also some glorious architecture as well as plenty of fish restaurants right by the water. **Heybeliada** offers similar attractions without the summer crowds, while **Burgazada** and **Kınalıada** are much smaller and easier to get round on foot. **Sedefadası** is virtually uninhabited but has a very exclusive restaurant.

YEDİKULE AND THE LAND WALLS

As you arrive in old İstanbul from Atatürk Airport you can hardly fail to spot the jagged remains of the old walls that defended Constantinople from attack by land until the months of April and May in 1453 when the Ottomans blasted their way through them to capture the city. The walls have been patched up over and again, and sporadic (and controversial) work still continues on them today. It's a long, hot but interesting walk north from **Yedikule (Seven Towers),** ①, the fortress close to the Sea of Marmara that is now a museum, to Ayvansaray where the land walls joined up with the sea walls guarding the city against attack from the Golden Horn. On the way you'll pass close to the **1453 Panorama Museum** ② at Topkapı, a new museum that attempts to recreate the day that Byzantine Constantinople was

Left: the Princes' Islands offers sunbathing opportunities.

VELİEFENDİ HIPPODROME

When it comes to sport people usually associate İstanbul most strongly with football. There is, however, a keen jockey club whose fans hang out in Bakırköy watching the races at the century-old **Veliefendi Hippodrome** ⑥.
SEE ALSO SPORT, P.105

ELGİZ MODERN ART GALLERY

The suburb of Maslak is mostly known for skyscrapers housing the headquarters of Turkey's biggest banks. However, tucked in amid all the naked commerce there's also a wonderful privately-run **art gallery** ⑦ which displays a series of everchanging exhibitions of paintings by the big names of the modern international art world.

BELGRADE FOREST

Named after the settlers brought here in the 15th century, the **Belgrade Forest** ④ is a vast tract of woodland to the northwest of İstanbul which is very popular as a summer picnic place with the locals. For those who like to combine sightseeing with al fresco dining the Forest is dotted with ancient aqueducts and reservoirs that form part of a complex network that still brings water into the city. Some of the aqueducts were designed by Sinan, the same great architect who was responsible for so many of the city mosques.
SEE ALSO PARKS, GARDENS AND BEACHES, P.97

BOSPHORUS ZOO

Since İstanbul is rather low on attractions designed specifically for children some parents may be relieved to learn that there is a small **zoo**, albeit way out at Gebze in the eastern outskirts. Note, however, that Turkey's treatment of animals is dismal and this can be a depressing place.
SEE ALSO CHILDREN, P.41

FORUM AQUARIUM

The vast Forum shopping centre near the main city bus terminal at Bayrampaşa incorporates a state-of-the art **aquarium** ⑤, another welcome break from historic sightseeing for hard-pressed parents.
SEE ALSO CHILDREN, P.41

Of İstanbul's three big football teams, the one whose stadium is the most out of the way for casual visitors is **Galatasaray** ('Cim Bom') who play at Aslantepe. *(See also Sport, p.104.)*

Below: passionate Galatasaray fans.

A–Z

In the following section İstanbul's attractions and services are organised by theme, under alphabetical headings. Items that link to another theme are cross-referenced. All sights that are plotted on the atlas section at the end of the book are given a page number and grid reference.

Architecture

I stanbul is home to some stunning architecture, particularly the early Ottoman mosques. The architectural genius Sinan stamped his mark not just on the religious buildings but also on the aqueducts, bridges and other structures. He nonetheless took some of his inspiration from the most influential survivor from Byzantine times, the church of Aya Sofya. In the 19th century the Balyan family adorned the city with florid palaces and mosques. There was a late flowering of architectural splendour in the early years of the Republic since when İstanbul has been in thrall to dull concrete.

BYZANTINE ARCHITECTURE

Byzantium gave rise to buildings that differ greatly from those of Western Christendom. The most important of all was the church of **Aya Sofya**, built by Emperor Justinian in 537 and adorned with a dome, dreamt up by Anthemius of Tralles and Isidore of Miletus, that was unique in its enormous size. All the churches that came after it included a dome although on a much smaller scale, and most were built in a basic cross shape of brick. Like Aya Sofya they were richly decorated with mosaics and frescoes; a Byzantine Renaissance of the 13th and 14th centuries had as its crowning glory the wonderful **Chora Church** near Edirnekapı.

There are plenty of Byzantine churches in old İstanbul although all except the Church of St Mary of the Mongols were converted into mosques

Above: in the Byzantine Aya Sofya.

after the Ottoman conquest of 1453. Less survives of Byzantine secular architecture. Beneath what is now Sultanahmet lie the remains of what must once have been a palace to equal Topkapı Sarayı in grandeur; today little more than the mosaic on display in the **Great Palace Mosaics Museum** survives to hint at what has been lost. The ancient cisterns such as the **Basilica**

Cistern are also venerable relics of Byzantine civic architecture.

SEE ALSO MONUMENTS, P.72; MOSQUES, SYNAGOGUES AND CHURCHES, P.78, 82

EARLY OTTOMAN ARCHITECTURE

When the Ottomans burst through the walls to seize Constantinople in 1453 they brought with them their own religion, Islam, and almost at once the old churches of Byzantium were converted into mosques by the simple expedient of adding minarets and replacing the altars with Mecca-facing *mihrabs*. Work also began immediately on creating new purpose-designed mosques. Two of the earliest were the **Fatih Mosque**, built over the site of the old Church of the Twelve Apostles, and the **Beyazıt Mosque**, near the Covered Bazaar. But it was the great architect Mimar Sinan (1489–1588) who perfected the design of the classic İstanbul

Left: elegant houses line the shores of the Bosphorus.

tecture, and they commissioned a series of ornate palaces from the prolific Armenian Balyan family of architects. The most important was **Dolmabahçe Palace**, which is designed in a style that strikes many modern visitors as overblown. Smaller and therefore sometimes easier to appreciate is the **Beylerbeyi Palace** on the Asian shore of the Bosphorus.
SEE PALACES, P.93, 95

FIRST NATIONAL ARCHITECTURE
As nationalism developed in Turkey towards the end of the 19th and early 20th centuries so a style of architecture intended to embody it also appeared. The brainchild particularly of Vedat Tek (1873–1942) and Kemaleddin Bey (1870–1927), First National Architecture featured thick lancet windows, overhanging roofs, and panels of Kütahya tiles on the exterior of buildings. Its finest exemplar in İstanbul is Tek's **Main Post Office** building in Sirkeci.

Art Nouveau had a flowering in late 19th and early 20th-century İstanbul especially under the tutelage of the Italian architect Raimondo d'Aronco whose **Casa Botter** on İstiklal Caddesi is one of its finest examples.

---

mosque with its multiple domes, graceful pencil minarets, large porticoed courtyard and a complex of associated buildings to house the soup kitchen, school, library etc. Sinan is credited with 42 mosques in İstanbul. His masterpiece is thought to

be the **Süleymaniye Mosque** although the nearby **Şehzade Mosque** gives it a run for its money in the beauty stakes.
SEE ALSO MOSQUES, SYNAGOGUES AND CHURCHES, P.79, 80

LATE OTTOMAN ARCHITECTURE
By the 19th century the Ottoman Empire was in such a fragile state that it was dubbed 'the Sick Man of Europe'. In an attempt to salvage the situation the later sultans turned to the West for models, not least in archi-

---

Below: the Aqueduct of Valens dates from Roman times.

If you take a cruise along the Bosphorus you will catch a glimpse many fine wooden mansions, called **yalıs**, that were built by the wealthy between the 18th and early 20th centuries. The majority have been lost to fire and other misfortunes; those that survive are sometimes called 'the pearls of the Bosphorus'. The oldest is the **Köprülü Amcazade Hüseyin Paşa Yalısı** at Anadolu Hisarı.

Bars and Cafés

Much of İstanbul's vibrancy comes from the existence of a seemingly limitless array of places to eat and drink including cafés offering everything from breakfast *böreks* (pastries) through light lunches and afternoons teas, to evening meals. Teahouses used to be men-only venues but in İstanbul this applies only in the most traditional neighbourhoods; elsewhere tea gardens, in particular, welcome all comers. In areas like Taksim it's hard to tell where a café ends and a bar begins. You'll have no trouble finding alcohol outside of conservative districts such as Fatih. *See also Nightlife, p.90.*

SULTANAHMET AND KUMKAPI

Café Meşale

Arasta Çarşısı 45; tel: 0212-518 9562; daily 24 hrs; tram: Sultanahmet; map p.121 D1
Immediately in front of the Arasta Bazaar in the shadow of the Blue Mosque, Meşale (Torch) has lots of outdoor tables with a choice of traditional stools or comfy armchairs where you can sip tea with the locals, try your hand at *tavla* (backgammon), puff on a *nargile* (waterpipe) or listen to live music.

Çiğdem Pastanesi

Divan Yolu 62/A; tel: 0212-526 8859; daily 8am–10pm; tram: Sultanahmet; map p.121 C2
A mouth-watering selection of cakes grabs the eye

In July 2009 smoking was banned in all covered venues in Turkey. This is fairly rigorously enforced in summer when everyone migrates outdoors anyway. In winter, it's more hit and miss, although you have a right to object to smokers.

of people strolling up and down Divan Yolu but there's also a great choice of pastries here too. The café has almost outgrown its premises although tables spill out onto the pavement in summer. Prices are very reasonable, hence the enthusiastic local clientele.

Dervish Aile Çay Bahçesi

Mimar Mehmet Ağa Caddesi, Sultanahmet; daily 9am–11pm; tram: Sultanahmet; map p.121 D1
When it's too hot to be indoors this tea garden across the road from the Blue Mosque offers lots of tables beneath shady plane trees where you can stick with a traditional tea or push the boat out with a smoothie to go with a light meal. In the evening a whirling dervish performs on stage here.

Şerbethane

Arasta Bazaar 117; tel: 0212-517 0004; www.serbethane. com; daily 8am–2am; tram: Sultanahmet, then 15-minute

Above: pouring some thick Turkish coffee.

walk; map p.121 D1
Housed in and around the remains of a forgotten Ottoman structure, this orientalist fantasy of a café attracts a lively crowd of locals who enjoy the tea and *nargiles*, as well as tourists who enjoy eating under the stars. The house speciality is a range of traditional sherbet drinks (cordials) that go well with snacks such as *gözleme* (Turkish pancakes).

Yeşil Ev Garden Café

Kabasakal Caddesi 5, Sultan-

Left: the stunning view from Pierre Loti Café.

tea-swilling students, this tea garden is shoehorned in between the buildings that used to house the social amenities attached to the Süleymaniye Mosque. Cafés don't get much more historic than this.

Şark Kahvesi

Yağlıkcılar Caddesi 134, Grand Bazaar; tel: 0212- 512 1144; Mon–Sat 8am–7pm; tram: Beyazıt/Kapalı Çarşı; map p.120 B2

Nicotine-coloured walls covered with images of Ottoman pashas and greased-up wrestlers give a cosily traditional feel to this long-standing café right inside the Grand Bazaar. It's strictly tea, coffee, cold drinks or fruit juices, but you won't need to take out a mortgage to buy them.

EMİNÖNÜ AND THE GOLDEN HORN
Pierre Loti Café

Gümüşsyu Caddesi, Balmumcu Sokak 5, Eyüp; tel: 0212-581 2696; daily 8am–midnight; ferry: Eyüp, the cable car

A tourist attraction-cum-café, the Pierre Loti stands

ahmet; tel: 0212-517 6785; daily noon–10.30pm; tram: Sultanahmet; map p.121 D2

A cut above most of the cafés and tea gardens is this delightful garden attached to a restored Ottoman house hotel that serves refreshments and drinks around a fountain.

BEYAZIT AND FATİH
Fes Café

Ali Baba Türbe Sokak 25-7, Nuruosmanye Caddesi, Beyazıt; tel: 0212-256 3070; www.fescafe.com; daily 8am–11pm; tram: Çemberlitaş; map p.120 C2

A delectable café that outgrew its original incar-

nation inside the Grand Bazaar (still doing good business), Fes mixes the kitsch (zebra head on the wall) with the stylish (fresh gladioli on the tables). A great selection of soups, salads and pastas come with a backdrop of anything from Abba to documentaries on the Black Sea on the plasma TV.

Lale Bahçesi

Sifahane Sokak, Süleymaniye; daily 8am–midnight; tram: Beyazıt, then 10-minute walk; map p.120 B3

Filled to the gunnels with

When you emerge exhausted from the Grand Bazaar you might be pleased to know that pedestrianised Nuruosmaniye Caddesi is a whole Coffee Alley of places to grab a quick drink and a bite to eat. Stick with the familiar at Starbucks, go local (and cheap) at Kahve Dünyası or dig your teeth into a plate of chewy Turkish ice cream (*Maraş dondurması*) at Mado.

Below: stopping for a tea break in the Grand Bazaar.

Left: unusual decor in Cafe Nar.

high on a hill overlooking the Bahariye (Navy) Islands at the far end of the Golden Horn. The French writer Pierre Loti used to frequent an earlier café on the site for its spectacular views. It's drinks and toast-style snacks only but the views remain the real draw.

Tahtakale Hamam Café
Uzun Çarşı Caddesi 329, Tahtakale; tel: 0212-514 4042; Mon–Sat 8am–10pm; tram: Eminönü, then 10-minute walk; map p.120 B3
Exotic café inside a disused 15th-century bathhouse. The juices are fresh, the ciabatta sandwiches delightful, and the low prices reflect a clientele that is still largely local.

BEYOĞLU
Badehane
General Yazgan Sokak 5, Tünel; tel: 0212-249 0550; daily 9am–2am; funicular: Tünel; map p.116 B2
Tucked into a grungy little alley that has been engulfed by recent gentrification, the Badehane still manages to feel like a local watering-hole first and foremost with prices a fraction of those at its glitzier neighbours.

Haco Pulo
İstiklal Caddesi, Hazzopolu Pasajı, Galatasaray; tel: 0212-244 4210; daily 9am–11pm; funicular: Tünel, then 10-minute walk; map p.116 B3
Trendy İstiklal Caddesi doesn't have much space these days for the old-fashioned glass of tea, so it's good to know that there is one traditional tea garden tucked out of sight across the road from the Yapı Kredi bookshop. Stools set round low tables on cobblestones – it could hardly get more Olde Turkey.

Kaktüs
İmam Adnan Sokak 4, Taksim; tel: 0212-249 5979; Mon–Sat

Ten years ago the *nargile*, or water-pipe, was on its last legs, smoked only by elderly men in flat caps in smoke-filled teahouses. In the last five years, however, it has come right back into fashion with all and sundry, and many cafes now emit the sweet scent of apple tobacco. One of the most atmospheric places to draw on a waterpipe is the Çorlulu Ali Paşa Medresesi on Divan Yolu, but for a great choice of places to smoke head straight for Tophane where behind the Nusretiye Mosque there's a whole cluster of *nargile* cafés.

9am–2am; funicular: Taksim; map p.116 C3
Cosy little bar with tables outside for sunny summer evenings and a Parisian feel to the wood-floored interior.

KeVe
Tünel Geçidi 10, Tünel; tel: 0212-251 4338; daily 8.30am–2am; funicular: Tünel; map p.116 B2
Tucked into an Art Nouveau arcade opposite the Tünel exit, KeVe (a play on *kahve*, the Turkish for coffee) is a fairy-tale venue with tiny lights strung through bushes creating a magical effect. The food is trendy fusion with salads and sandwiches to go alongside the coffee, cakes and alcohol, but this is predominantly a place to come for the setting.

Molly's Café
Camekan Sokak 10; tel: 0212-245 1696; daily 10am–10pm; funicular: Tünel; map p.116 B1
Homely little café in trendy Kuledibi which offers coffee, cakes and a range of other soft drinks, as well as themed dinners, poetry readings, book signings,

Below: in local's favourite, the Badehane.

Sprawling café with lots of outdoor tables as well as a large indoor seating area that is handy for the Sakıp Sabancı Museum. Prices are very low for a menu that offers everything from *balkaymak* (honey and cream) breakfasts to a standard range of kebabs.

etc. Internet access, board games and a book exchange add to the attractions.

THE BOSPHORUS

Aşşk Kahve
Muallim Naci Caddesi 648, Kuruçeşme; tel: 0212-265 4734; daily 9am–10pm; bus: 25RE from Kabataş
Classic brunching establishment in a narrow strip of land running down to the Bosphorus beside the large Macro Center. The food here is as fresh as it comes and the choice of everything down to bread is matchless. You'll be lucky to get a table over summer weekends.

Cafe Nar
Yahya Kemal Caddesi 16/B, Rumeli Hisarı; tel: 0212-263 2446; www.cafenar.com; daily 8am–midnight; bus: 25RE from Kabataş
Excellent breakfasts and wonderful fresh juices at this delightful small café overlooking the Bosphorus. *Nar* is Turkish for pomegranate, hence that fruit's frequent apearance on the menu.

Happily Ever After
Cevdetpaşa Caddesi 24/A, Bebek; tel: 0212-263 4138; daily 8am–midnight; bus: 25RE from Kabataş

Waterside café with pavement tables and a feminine feel. Cup cakes, real pancakes and all sorts of other fresh bakery goods available all day alongside health-conscious smoothies.

Sade Kahve
Yahya Kemal Caddesi 36, Rumeli Hisarı; tel: 0212-358 2324; www.sadekahve.com; daily 8am–2am; bus: 25RE from Kabataş
In the shadow of Rumeli Hisarı looking straight over the Bosphorus this hugely popular café is especially popular for Sunday brunch; come then for the buzz or pick a quieter time to enjoy the rest of a menu which majors on sandwiches and salads.

Sütiş
Sakıp Sabancı Caddesi 1/3, Emirgan; tel: 0212-323 5030; daily 8am–midnight; bus: 25RE from Kabataş

Pudding shops were once a distinctive part of İstanbul life catering to those whose sweet tooth craved milk puddings in particular. Recently they have undergone a revival, with the Özsüt chain of cafés once again dispensing *sütlaç* (rice pudding) alongside the gateaux and biscuits.

Taps
Cevdetpaşa Caddesi 119, Bebek; tel: 0212-263 8700; www.tapsbebek.com; daily noon–1am; bus: 25RE from Kabataş
This is a water-facing branch of a small microbrewery offering one of the best choices of beer in İstanbul.

KADIKÖY AND ÜSKÜDAR

Baylan Pastanesi
Muvakkithane Caddesi 19, Kadıköy; tel: 0216-336 2881; www.baylanpastanesi.com; daily 10am–10pm; ferry: Kadıköy, then 10-minute walk
Old-fashioned cake shop with a small garden at the back where those in the know tuck into the Cup Griye, an ice-cream sundae with lashings of caramel.

GREATER İSTANBUL

Kahve Dünyası
23 Nisan Caddesi 32, Büyükada; tel: 0216-382 8399; www.kahvedunyasi.com; daily 9am–10pm; ferry: Büyükada
Kahve Dünyası is the Turkish take on Starbucks and its flagship café is poised in front of the Splendid Hotel to soak up the splendid view back towards mainland Turkey. The menu is similar to Starbucks' but for roughly half the price.

Bazaars and Shopping

For many visitors a trip to İstanbul's historic Grand Bazaar is second in importance only to Topkapı Palace. This vast undercover shopping emporium has a smaller counterpart in the Egyptian or Spice Market, now increasingly given over to souvenirs. Locals still go to the Grand Bazaar to buy gold for wedding presents, and to the area around the Spice Market to shop for fruit and vegetables. Otherwise most shopping goes on it one of the vast malls that have sprung up over the last five years.

ANTIQUES

Before snapping up anything truly old in Turkey you need to know that the laws on exporting antiques are extremely strict; nothing more than a hundred years old can be taken out of the country without authority on pain of a jail sentence.

SULTANAHMET AND KUMKAPI

Khaftan
Nakilbent Sokak 33, Tel: 0212-458 5425, www.khaftan.com; daily 9am–8pm; tram: Sultanahmet; map p.121 C1

In Turkey bargaining (*pazarlık* in Turkish) has more or less died a death unless you are buying in bulk. In the İstanbul bazaars, however, it still lives on and you would be ill-advised ever to pay the first price requested. The rule of thumb is to offer around 50 per cent and then negotiate upwards, but in the case of items such as silver jewellery you can only really barter over the cost of the labour since the price of precious metals is fixed every day.

Above: an artisan at work making ceramic pots.

Aladdin's cave of a shop full of old paintings, costumes, postcards, books, statues, jewellery and assorted curios.

BEYAZIT AND FATİH

Horhor Antique Centre
Horhor Antıkıcılar Çarşısı, Horhor Caddesi, Tulumba Kırma Sokak, Aksaray; tel: varies with shops; www.horhor.com; Mon–Sat 9am–6pm; tram: Aksaray, then 15-minute walk; map p.119 E3

In 1981 a fire in Kuledibi forced the antique dealers of Galata to relocate to this grim building which contains, nonetheless, seven wonderful floors of antiques and collectibles. Few bargains, but the best choice in the city.

Sofa
Nuruosmaniye Caddesi 85, Nuruosmaniye; tel: 0212-520 2850; www.kashifsofa.com; daily 9.30am–7pm; tram: Çemberlitaş; map p.120 C2

It may be outside the Grand Bazaar but this corner shop has such an eye-catching array of antiquities and paintings in its windows that you won't be able to stop yourself from pulling out your wallet again.

BEYOĞLU

Artrium
Tünel Geçidi 7, Tünel; tel: 0212-251 4302; daily 10am–7pm; funicular: Tünel; map p.116 B2

Fancy an Ottoman print to take home? Or a single beautiful antique tile? Then this glorious Aladdin's Cave of a shop will be the place for you.

CARPETS AND TEXTILES
Turkey is famous for its carpet shops as well as for

Left: the Grand Bazaar, an unmissable experience.

Shops are also listed elsewhere in the guide. For clothing, see *Fashion, p.46;* for beauty products, see *Hamams and Spas, p.56;* for food, see *Food and Drink, p.52;* for books, see *Literature, p.71.*

Look out too for rich, heavy Uzbek velvets as well as thick denim-blue quilts from Iran.

Sedir

Mimar Mehmed Ağa Caddesi 39, Sultanahmet; tel: 0212-516 8045; daily 9am–6pm; tram: Sultanahmet, then 10-minute walk; map p.121 D1

Carpet shop spread over several floors that specializes in kilims (flat weaves) but also offers a wide range of carpets, including many from Iran and Pakistan.

BEYAZIT AND FATİH

Punto

Gazi Sinan Paşa Sokak, Vezirhan 17, Nuruosmaniye; tel: 0212-511 0853; daily 9am–8m; tram: Çemberlitaş; map p.120 C2

This is a reliable and high-quality carpet shop housed inside an ancient *han* just outside the Grand Bazaar.

the hard-sell that often accompanies shopping in them. Take your time, don't fall for any flannel, and you can have a great time looking around. Bear in mind that most of the pieces on sale will have come from elsewhere in the Islamic world, and that some of the nomadic pieces represent especially good value for money as the way of life that produced them is on its very last legs.

SULTANAHMET AND KUMKAPI

Cocoon

Arasta Bazaar 93; tel: 0212-638 6450; www.cocoontr.com; daily 8.30am–7.30pm; tram: Sultanahmet, then 10-minute walk; map p.121 D1

You won't be able to miss this shop whose windows are full of colourful felt hats in a multitude of shapes as well as a range of shawls so fine that it's hard to believe that they too are made from felt. Continue down Küçük Ayasofya Caddesi to find two more shops in the same stable that stock carpets, textiles and yet more felty artefacts.

Mehmet Çetinkaya Gallery

Tavukhane Sokak, Sultanahmet; tel: 0212-517 6808; www.cetinkayagallery.com; daily 9.30am–7.30pm; tram: Sultanahmet, then 10-minute walk; map p.121 D1

Collector's carpet and textile shop par excellence where you're guaranteed to find pieces unavailable elsewhere such as stunning and colourful *kaitag* embroideries from Daghestan in the Caucasus.

Below: a Turkish rug is a classic buy.

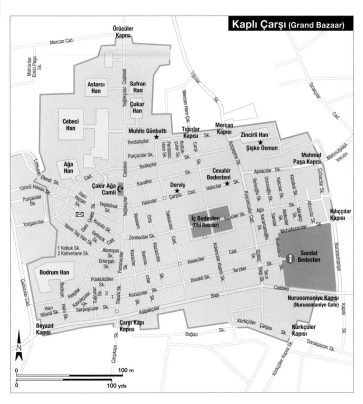

Kaplı Çarşı (Grand Bazaar)

Şişko Osman

Zincirli Han 15, Grand Bazaar; tel: 0212-528 3548; Mon–Sat 9am–7pm; tram: Beyazıt; map p.120 C2

Tucked away in one of the prettiest corners of the Grand Bazaar, 'Fatty Osman's' has been in business for four generations, which means that the staff really know how to separate the deep-pile

carpets from the also-ran floor coverings.

CERAMICS
ATA Quartz

Arasta Bazaar 57; tel: 0212-517 3022; daily 10am–8pm; tram: Sultanahmet, then 10-minute walk; map p.121 D1

Long-established shop selling quartz-clay ceramics and some red-clay ware from Avanos in Cappadocia. Some of the work is by less well-known artists resulting in relatively low prices.

İznik Classics

Utangaç Sokak 17, Sultanahmet; tel: 0212-516 7473; daily 10am–8pm; tram: Sultanahmet, then 10-minute walk; map p.121 D1

This shop, with a second branch in the Grand Bazaar, stocks all manner of plates, bowls and jugs, some with original İznik designs, some with a more contemporary look.

Nakkaş

Nakilbent Sokak 30; tel: 0212-516 5222; www.nakkasrug. com; daily 9am–7pm; tram: Sultanahmet, then 10-minute walk; map p.121 C1

A carpet-cum-jewellery shop perched above the remains of a sixth-century cistern, Nakkaş also stocks a range of ceramics made by the İznik Foundation, the organisation that was responsible for reviving the İznik tiles that are the glory

Bağdat Caddesi in Kadıköy is Asia's answer to İstiklal Caddesi just with the historic buildings removed and the nostalgic tram replaced with a tourist-unfriendly one-way traffic system. Full of familiar international brand names, it's not an exciting place to shop. On the other hand it's calm and spacious, with lots of banks and coffee shops to ease the business of parting with your cash.

of so many 16th and 17th-century mosques.

Above: slippers for sale in the Grand Bazaar.

GRAND BAZAAR
Kapalı Çarşı, Ordu Caddesi, Beyazıt; tel: 0212-514 0045; www.grandbazaar.com; Mon–Sat 9am–7pm; tram: Beyazıt/Kapalı Çarşı; map p.120 C2

With a reputed 4,000 shops crammed together beneath one roof, the Grand or Covered Bazaar is the ultimate İstanbul shopping experience, albeit one that can sometimes leave you longing for the calm detachment of a mall.

'Twas ever thus though as Mark Twain was complaining about the touts as long ago as 1867, so your best bet is to step smart, keep an eye on your purse and try to keep a smile on your face even when you hear the same 'joke' for the fifteenth time.

With so many shops to choose from it can be hard to know where to start. Here are a few suggestions – and don't forget that some of the most atmospheric places to explore are the crumbling *hans* on the fringes of the bazaar where, in the past, traders and their animals would have put up for the night.

Adıyaman Pazarı
Yağlıkcılar Caddesi 74–6; tel: 0212-526 9759

Wonderful fabric shop full of the rusty-coloured, striped *kutnu* textiles traditionally used for robes in Gaziantep in southeastern Turkey.

Ak Gümüş
Gani Çelebi Sokak 8; tel: 0212-526 0987

Sells round red and black wooden boxes from Türkmenistan and felt figurines imported from Kyrgyzstan as part of a CASCA (Central Asian Crafts Support Association) project aimed at reviving indigenous handicrafts.

Muhlis Günbattı
Perdahçılar Sokak 48; tel: 0212-511 6562

Gorgeous Ottoman fabrics, old dowry boxes, antique jewellery – a real treasure chest of a store.

HANDICRAFTS

SULTANAHMET AND KUMKAPI

İkonium
Küçük Ayasofya Caddesi 80/2, Sultanahmet; tel: 0532-698 2824; www.thefeltmaker.net; daily 10am–8pm; tram: Sultanahmet, then 20-minute walk; map p.121 C1

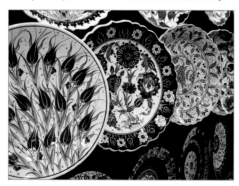

Left: painted ceramics make an excellent souvenir.

35

Tucked up beneath İstiklal Caddesi in Beyoğlu, Çukurcuma is one of the best places in the city to shop for antiques. One of the most romantic shops is Leyla (Altı Patlar Sokağı 6A) which is stuffed full with gorgeous embroideries from all over the country. Look for the London Transport request bus stop to find Üsküdarlı Bayram (Faikpaşa Caddesi 26A) which sells everything from bric-a-brac to valuable antiques. Kuti Retromodern (Faikpaşa Caddesi 51A) shows off all sorts of snazzy lighting, while Roman (Ağa Hamam Sokak 34) reconditions everything from old milk churns to broken-down chairs.

Great place to come to learn about felt-making and to buy felt rugs with contemporary designs.

İstanbul Handicrafts Centre
Kabasakal Caddesi 23, Sultanahmet; tel: 0212-517 6782; daily 9am–6.30pm; tram: Sultanahmet; map p.121 D2
Housed in what were the students' rooms at the Kabasakal Medresesi (seminary), this pretty little craft centre is a good place to find out about calligraphy, miniature-painting, marbling, glasswork and other traditional crafts.

Martı
Küçük Ayasofya Camii Sokak 12/A, Sultanahmet; tel: 0212-458 5164; daily 10am–8pm; tram: Sultanahmet, then 20-minute walk; map p.121 C1
Small workshop where old print-making techniques are being given new life. Come here to stock up on cushion covers, wall hangings, even blouses.

THE BOSPHORUS
Every Sunday a handicrafts market fills the streets running down to the water at Ortaköy. It kicks off around 10am and ends around 8pm in summer, and is a great place to stock up on hand-made jewellery, novelty hats, children's toys and myriad other delights.

JEWELLERY

BEYAZIT AND FATİH
Design Zone
Alibaba Türbe Sokak 21, Nuruosmaniye; tel; 0212-527 9285; www.designzone.com; Mon–Sat 10am–6pm; tram: Çemberlitaş; map p.120 C2
This shop has a wide choice of one-off designs to suit all budgets.

Sevan Bıçakçı
Gazi Sinan Paşa Sokak 16, Nuruosmaniye; tel: 0212-520 4516; www.sevanbicakci.com; daily 10am–6pm; tram: Çemberlitaş; map p.121 C2
If money's no object, İstanbul's own 'Lord of the Rings' Sevan Bıçakçı is sure to have made a piece of jewellery to leave you drooling and reaching for the credit card.

BEYOĞLU
Aida Pekin
Serdar-ı Ekrem Caddesi 44/A, Galata; tel: 0212-243 1211; Mon–Sat 11am–7pm; funicular: Tünel; map.116 B2
Cute little corner shop full of one-off designs drawn from popular landmarks such as the nearby Galata Tower that make perfect souvenirs or gifts.

MALLS
İstanbul's first shopping mall, Galleria at Bakırköy, still lives on but since it was built in 1988 the world of

Above: an enticing treasure trove of jewellery.

Turkish retail has undergone a drastic transformation and now barely a day passes but that there's news of a new mall (*alışveriş merkezi* or AVM in Turkish) opening. In these somewhat strange places you could sometimes be forgiven for completely forgetting that you were in Turkey, especially as you walk past a familiar line-up of Marks & Spencer, Body Shop, Mothercare and Claire's Accessories. On the other hand, it's sometimes comforting to be able to shop away from the traffic in air-conditioned comfort.

NİŞANTAŞI, TEŞVIKIYE AND MAÇKA
City's Shopping Mall
Teşvikiye Caddesi 162, Nişantaşı; tel: 0212-373 3333; www.citynisantasi.com; daily 10am–10pm; Metro: Osmanbey
Neither the biggest nor the flashiest of İstanbul's malls, City's is nevertheless easy to get to by public transport and houses a reasonable range of chain labels as well as a small basement food hall.

GREATER İSTANBUL
Forum Shopping Centre
Paşa Caddesi, Kocatepe; tel:

0212-443 1350; www.forumİstanbul.com; daily 10am–10pm; tram: Kartaltepe/Kocatepe

Newest of the shopping malls is this sprawling endeavour squeezed in between a branch of IKEA and İstanbul's Esenler bus station. Wide walkways and some inviting outdoor café areas, as well as the Turkuazoo aquarium make this a great place to shop for all Turkey's high-street labels as well as Marks & Spencer et al.

Above: the modern Kanyon shopping centre.

İstinye Park

İstinye Bayırı Caddesi, İstinye; tel: 0212-345 5555; www.istinyepark.com; daiy 10am–10pm; Metro: İTU Ayazağa

Uber-glitzy shopping mall with a wonderful food hall mildly reminiscent of Harrods that is surrounded by great places to eat.

Kanyon

Büyükdere Caddesi 185, Levent; tel: 0212-353 5300; www.kanyon.com.tr; daily 10am–10pm; Metro: Şişli-Mecidiyeköy

The most architecturally interesting of the malls, not least because it is partly open to the elements, Kanyon caters for a well-heeled clientele which means a big Harvey Nichols, an Apple Store and a string of high-quality restaurants. Too pricy for you? Then pop into Metrocity right next door.

MUSIC

If you are looking for something to play rather than listen to then Galipdede Caddesi in Tünel is lined with shops selling musical instruments.

BEYOĞLU

Lale Plak

Galipdede Caddesi 1, Tünel: tel: 0212-293 7739; Mon–Sat 9am–7pm; funicular: Tünel; map p.116 B2

Tired of the same old range of pop CDs? Then head straight for this famous small store that is crammed with recordings of everything from jazz through folk to Turkish classical music.

SPICE MARKET

Mısır Çarşısı, Eminönü; Mon–Sat 8.30am–6.30pm, also Sun from mid-Jun to mid-Sept; tram: Eminönü; map p.120 C3

Fancy some saffron, cloves or cinnamon to take home with you? Then home in on the atmospheric Spice (Egyptian) Market dating back to 1660 that sits beside the New Mosque (Yeni Camii) where stalls selling herbs and spices are now interspersed with those selling souvenir tea sets and *nargiles*. Shops worth making a beeline for include Kalmaz Baharat (tel: 0212-522 6604) and Özer (tel: 0212-526 8079), the latter stocking luxurious textiles rather than spices.

Below: sweet things piled up in the Spice Market.

Immediately beside the Spice Market is Tahtakale, a wonderful maze of tight-knit shopping streets dating back to the Middle Ages. Come here to shop for everything from hardware and board games to sweets and coffee with the locals. In the weeks leading up to the end of December it's a great place to shop for cheap Christmas decorations – which the Turks use to celebrate the New Year (*Yılbaşı*).

Boat Trips

İstanbul's location not just on the Bosphorus but also on the Sea of Marmara means that no matter where you are in the old or new city a watery view is rarely more than a stroll away. And what you see when you gaze out on the water is an extraordinary array of passing boats in every shape and size. There are the huge tankers that use the Bosphorus to get from the Black Sea to the Sea of Marmara; there are the ferries that criss-cross the Bosphorus throughout the day; and there are the hundreds of pleasure craft that enable people to cruise around the city without having to worry about the traffic.

Above: it is possible to rent private boats too.

For information about local ferry services, see Transport, p.106.

LONG BOSPHORUS CRUISES

İstanbul Deniz Otobüsleri (İDO), Eminönü; tel: 0212-444 4436; www.ido.com.tr; tram: Eminönü; map p.121 C4

On a summer day few things could be more enjoyable than to embark on one of İDO's three times daily sailings all the way along the Bosphorus from Eminönü to Anadolu Kavağı at the mouth of the Black Sea. The boats leave at 10.35am, noon (summer only) and 1.35pm, and demand is high so it's advisable to arrive a good half-hour early to be sure of a decent seat. It takes an hour and a half to reach Anadolu Kavağı, and on the way there you will be able to see some of the city's greatest monuments such as the Dolmabahçe and Beylerbeyi Palaces, and the Rumeli Hisarı and Anadolu Hisarı fortresses from the water, which is how they would have been accessed originally. You will also be able to see some of the wonderful wooden *yalıs* (waterfront mansions) that have survived the ravages of time to become some of İstanbul's most valuable real estate.

The ferries stop at Beşiktaş, Kanlıca, Yeniköy, Sarıyer, Rumeli Kavağı and Anadolu Kavağı. Leave the boat either at Rumeli Kavağı or Anadolu Kavağı to indulge in a fish lunch before the return journey. Most people prefer to get out at Anadolu Kavağı since it's possible to climb the hill there to Yoros Kalesi (Yoros Castle) and a panoramic view of the Bosphorus and the Black Sea. Be sure to buy a carton of creamy Kanlıca yoghurt from the crew on the return journey since its production is a specialty of the suburb.

Left: Bosphorus ferries dock at several photogenic points.

PRIVATE BOAT TRIPS

If you stroll along the waterfront between Bebek and Rumeli Hisarı you will see many boats lined up for individual hire. Negotiate with their owners over how long you will be on the water and on what route to take but don't expect prices to be particularly low.

SHORT BOSPHORUS CRUISES

If time is tight you might prefer to opt for one of the cruises offered by private operators at Eminönü. They sail as far as the first Bosphorus Bridge before turning round again and don't offer the option of disembarking along the way but the journey is very enjoyable nonetheless.

SUNSET (MEHTAP) CRUISES

İstanbul Deniz Otobüsleri (İDO), Eminönü; tel: 0212-444 4436; www.ido.com.tr; tram: Eminönü; Jul–Aug Sat 7.15pm map p.121 C4

In Ottoman times moonlit cruises were extremely popular, so what could be nicer than to take to the water as the sun is setting in emulation of the sultans? The route is much the same as for the long Bosphorus cruises and you'll be back at Eminönü around 11.30pm.

GOLDEN HORN CRUISES

İstanbul Deniz Otobüsleri (İDO), Eminönü; tel: 0212-444 4436; www.ido.com.tr; tram: Eminönü; map p.121 C4

The Golden Horn is a wonderful waterway to cruise along, and from the decks of the ferries you'll be able to see buildings such as the huge red-brick Fener High School for Boys and the newly restored Bahariye (Naval) Palace that are much harder to see close up. The ferries stop at Kasımpaşa, Fener, Hasköy, Ayvansaray, Sütlüce and Eyüp. The best places to disembark are Fener (for the Greek Patriarchate), Hasköy (for the Rahmi M. Koç Museum), Ayvansaray (for the city walls), Sütlüce (for Miniatürk and Santral-Istanbul) and Eyüp (for the Eyüp Sultan Mosque and Pierre Loti Café).

SEE ALSO BARS AND CAFÉS, P.29; CHILDREN, P.40; MONUMENTS, P.77; MOSQUES, SYNAGOGUES AND CHURCHES, P.80; MUSEUMS AND GALLERIES, P.86

Below: a ferry returns to İstanbul at sunset.

If time doesn't permit a proper cruise, then make sure to take a 'poor man's cruise' on one of the normal ferries, perhaps from Eminönü to Üsküdar or Kadıköy, to get a taste of the magic of the Bosphorus.

39

Children

Istanbul is hardly overrun with attractions purpose-designed to appeal to children. Nor are facilities for looking after them always as highly developed as elsewhere. On the other hand most Turks genuinely love children and bringing yours with you is likely to add to rather than detract from your trip. The situation is, in any case, fast improving. Many restaurants now have high chairs available, more public toilets have baby-changing facilities, and pavements are being relaid so getting about with a buggy is becoming easier. A growing number of play areas can also be found in the malls and public parks.

BABYSITTING

Most four and five-star hotels will be able to help you arrange a babysitter, although cheaper hotels may not. Children are prized in Turkey and restaurants waiters are often happy to help out with childcare unless they're extremely busy.

MINIATÜRK

İmrahor Caddesi, Sütlüce; tel: 0212-222 2882; www.minia turk.com.tr; 9am–6pm; charge; ferry: Sütlüce or bus 36T from

Below: in the İstanbul Archeology Museum.

Taksim
The jury is out on how much this collection of cut-down versions of all Turkey's most famous attractions actually appeals to children, but it is one of the very few city attractions that does at least seem to have been designed with them in mind and might well be fun if you are not going to be seeing the originals. It might be best to come by ferry to make it feel more of an occasion.

MUSEUMS

SULTANAHMET AND KUMKAPI

İstanbul Archeology Museum
Osman Hamdi Bey Yokuşu, Gül-hane Park; tel: 0212-520 7740; Tue–Sun 9am–5pm; charge; tram: Gülhane; map p.121 D2
There is a small children's section inside the main building of the İstanbul Archeology Museum. While the scenes of Anatolian life are not wildly exciting, it will at least amuse children too young to appreciate the main exhibits – and there's a fine model of the Trojan Horse to climb into too.
SEE ALSO MUSEUMS AND GALLERIES, P.84

EMİNÖNÜ AND THE GOLDEN HORN

Rahmi M. Koç Museum
Hasköy Caddesi 5; tel: 0212-369 6600; www.rmk-museum. org.tr; Tue–Fri 10am–5pm, Sat–Sun 10am–7pm; charge; ferry: Hasköy or bus 36T from Taksim; map p.115 C4
Housed in an old anchor-making factory and the

Left: a couple of local youngsters.

GREATER İSTANBUL

Göztepe Toy Museum
Göztepe Oyuncak Müzesi, Ömerpaşa Caddesi, Dr. Zeki Zeren Sokak, Göztepe; tel: 0216-359 4550; www.İstanbul-oyuncukmuzesi.com; Tue–Sun 10am–5pm; charge; train: Göztepe
Look out for the giraffe-shaped lamp posts to find this delightful museum housed inside a lovely old wooden house. Toys in all shapes and sizes can be found, and even the toilets have been designed to imitate a submarine. Out-size statues of Turkish folk heroes Nasreddin Hoca and Keloğlan ('the Bald Boy') stand in the grounds.

WILDLIFE ATTRACTIONS

GREATER İSTANBUL

Bosphorus Zoo
Bayramoğlu, Gebze; tel: 0262-653 1374; www.bosphoruszoo.com.tr; daily 9am–7pm; charge; train: Gebze, then local bus
Although Turkish zoos are more like concentration camps for animals than wildlife refuges (more sensitive children will find them depressing), local children seem to enjoy messing about in the giant outdoor playground here.

Turkuazoo
Forum Shopping Centre, Karatepe; tel: 0212-640 2740; www.turkuazoo.com; Mon–Fri 10am–7pm, Sat–Sun 10am–8pm; charge; tram: Kartaletepe/Kocatepe
The sharks may be the showstoppers at this new and excellent aquarium but really it's the leopard-patterned giant rays that will steal many visitors' hearts.

Most children will enjoy the ferry ride to Haydarpaşa station which passes a long breakwater usually covered in cormorants with their wings spread to catch the sun. Do like the locals and grab a *simit* (sesame-seed roll) before boarding to feed to the gulls who follow the boats.

---

grounds of a disused shipyard, the Rahmi M. Koç is a state-of-the art privately-run museum which boasts an astonishing array of preserved cars, boats, trains and trams guaranteed to appeal to children. There are reconstructed shops, the chance to dive below the Golden Horn in a submarine and to board an old steam train to chug a little way along the shore.

Türkiye İş Bankası Museum
Hamidiye Caddesi, Eminönü; Tue–Sun 9am–5pm; free; tram: Eminönü; map p.121 C3
A museum of banking might not sound a bundle of laughs for children, but in the case of the Türkiye İş Bankası Museum the basement is a revelation as you can walk right inside the old bank vaults as well as eyeball a selection of private safeboxes opened to show off the variety of items people thought worth paying to safeguard, including some toys.

NİŞANTAŞI, TEŞVİKYE AND MAÇKA

Military Museum
Askeri Müzesi, Valikonağı Caddesi, Harbiye; tel: 0212-233 2720; Wed–Sun 9am–5pm; charge; Metro: Osmanbey
While some of the battle details may be less than gripping, the Military Museum does contain such bloodthirsty items as a bullet-riddled car in which a politician was assassinated that will fascinate a number of children. Better still, it is the site every day at 3pm of loud performances by an Ottoman Mehter Band in wonderfully colourful costumes.

41

Essentials

When is the best time to visit İstanbul? Well, May to June and September to October offer the best combination of warm but not excessively hot or cold weather and less crowding. In July and August temperatures can soar to 35°C (95°F), and the crowds and traffic can make it seem even hotter; best, then, to pick a hotel as close to the sights as possible, and spend as much time as possible out on the Bosphorus. April is one of the busiest months for visitors but mid-month the Tulip Festival brings radiant colour to all the city's parks, a treat well worth grabbing.

BUSINESS HOURS

Government officials stick to a fairly standard 8.30am to 5pm working day with an hour off for lunch, and this applies to state-run museums and monuments too. Everyone else works from the minute they get out of bed to the time that the last possible customer has gone home again. Museums usually close on Mondays, government offices on Saturday and Sunday.

Above: ATMs are not hard to find.

CUSTOMS

There is no limit on the amount of foreign currency that can be brought into the country but no more than US$35,000 worth of Turkish lira can be taken in or out. You can take the following when you leave Turkey: 200 cigarettes, 10 cigars, two bottles of wine, 1kg of coffee and 0.5kg of tea. Check www.gumruk.gov.tr for full details.

ELECTRICITY

Turkey operates on a 220-volt, 50-cycle current. An adaptor for Continental-style two-pin sockets will be needed. American 110-volt appliances will also require a transformer.

EMBASSIES AND CONSULATES

The embassies are in Ankara but most countries also have consulates in İstanbul:

Australian Consulate: Tepecik Yolu 58, Etiler; tel: 0212-257 7050

British Consulate: Meşrutiyet Caddesi 34, Tepebaşı, Beyoğlu; tel:

0212-334 6400

Canadian Consulate: İstiklal Caddesi 375/5, Beyoğlu; tel: 0212-251 9838

US Consulate: Kaplıcalar Mavkii 2, İstinye; tel: 0212-335 9000

HEALTH

İstanbul is a fairly healthy city to visit, the main risks usually coming from exposure to the sun and the occasional dodgy food or drink item. Slap on the sun block and wear a hat during the summer, and be

Left: the helpful Tourist Information office.

speaking pharmacy in Sultanahmet on Divan Yolu (tel: 0212-513 5035).

Pharmacies rotate their night shifts and Sunday opening. A notice in the window should show the address of the nearest pharmacy that will be open (*nobetci*).

INTERNET ACCESS
The Turks took to the internet at the first opportunity and the streets used to be carpeted with internet cafés. Today they have largely disappeared because most hotels offer either in-house internet access or wi-fi, or both. Branches of Starbucks among other places also offer free wi-fi access to their customers. Internet cafés rarely charge more than 1TL per half-hour.

MEDIA AND LOCAL LISTINGS PAPERS
Television: State-owned TRT (Türkiye Radyo ve Televizyon) broadcasts several nationwide channels.

The three main **emergency numbers** in Turkey are:
Police: 155
Ambulance: 112
Fire: 110

---

careful with food, especially if uncooked and bought from street vendors in high summer.

Healthcare and insurance: Since there is no free healthcare for visitors, you should take out adequate insurance, preferably covering the cost of an emergency flight home in the event of serious injury or illness. However, if you don't have insurance İstanbul's private hospitals generally offer excellent standards of treatment and are not usually cripplingly expensive.

Vaccinations: Although there are no compulsory inoculation requirements you might want to consider up-to-date vaccinations for tetanus, polio, typhoid and hepatitis A.

Hospitals and pharmacies: The American Hospital (Amerikan Hastanesi; Güzelbahçe Sokak 20, Nişantaşi; tel: 0212-311 2000) is a good, clean and efficient hospital with English-speaking staff.

Pharmacies are indicated with a neon-lit 'E' sign. The Aykut Eczanesi is a 24-hour pharmacy in Taksim (Sıraselviler Caddesi 135; tel: 0212-243 1785), and there's a good English-

Below: the choice of papers includes English-language options.

News in English is shown at 10.30pm on TRT2, while international sports events can be watched on TRT3. Many hotels have satellite or cable television with BBC World, CNN and Al Jazeera plus German, French and other European channels.

Radio: The BBC World Service and Voice of America are available on shortwave radio. There are regular news summaries in English on TRT3 (88.4, 94.0 and 99.0 MHZ).

Newspapers: The English-language *Today's Zaman* and *Hurriyet Daily News* are published daily and offer national and international news and features. You can usually buy British newspapers in Sultanahmet and Taksim although they will be a day late and very expensive. *Time Out İstanbul in English* is the city's excellent monthly listings magazine.

MONEY

Currency: The Turkish currency is the Turkish Lira (TL). At the time of writing –although this can change quickly – £1 was equiva-

lent to TL2.30 and $1 to TL1.10. Coins come in 5, 10 and 25 kuruş and TL1 denominations. Notes come in 5, 10, 20, 50, 100 and 200 TL units.

Banks and currency exchange: Banks are usually open Mon–Fri 8.30am–5pm. The most efficient are Yapı Kredi, Garanti Bankası, HSBC and Akbank, although queues can be long and you can't assume on English-speaking staff. Rates of exchange and commission vary considerably, so you may want to shop around a bit. The rate in Turkey is always better than you would get in the UK so don't change your money into lira before arriving at the airport. You can also change cash at the post office. Almost no one uses traveller's cheques these days, so if you do bring them expect delays in cashing them.

Cash machines: ATM machines are liberally dotted about the city, with a rank of them in Sultahahmet Square. It's much quicker and easier to use a debit or credit card in an

ATM machine than to queue in the bank or post office to change your money.

Credit cards: Major credit cards (except American Express) are usually accepted by hotels, restaurants, tourist shops and car-hire companies. Some shops add a small premium to cover the cost of the card company's commission.

Exchange rates: To find out the day's exchange rates go to www.xe.com.

Taxes: VAT (KDV in Turkish) is charged at anything from 8 to 25 per cent on purchased goods. Foreigners are entitled to a refund on larger payments and some stores can provide paperwork which in theory enables you to reclaim the KDV at the airport; look for decals in their windows.

POST

Post offices (*postane* or *PTT* in Turkish) handle mail, parcels, and currency exchange. Usually there are phone boxes outside as well. Post offices are usually open Mon–Sat 9am–5pm. Sending a parcel sometimes involves irritating red tape; if so, try using one of the international courier companies instead.

The main post office in İstanbul is in Büyük Postane Caddesi (turn left, facing the ferries, at Sirkeci tram stop); other handy branches are inside the Grand Bazaar and in Galatasaray Square, off İstiklal Caddesi.

Stamps (*pul*) can be bought at shops selling postcards to avoid queu-

Left: Turkish currency.

Above: round up tips for taxi drivers to the nearest lira.

ing in the post office. You usually have to post your mail at the post office although you can also post it at the booth in Sultanahmet Square. There are two slots marked *yurtiçi* for destinations within Turkey; and *yurtdişi* for international mail. To send a 50g letter or a postcard from Turkey to the UK or US costs TL1.10.

TELEPHONES
The dialing code for Turkey is +90. For intercity calls (including calls to the Asian side of the Bosphorus) dial 0, then the area code (212 for European İstanbul, 216 for the Asian side), then the number. To make an international call, dial 00, then the country code (44 for the UK, 353 for Ireland, 1 for the US and Canada, 61 for Australia, 64 for New Zealand), followed by the area code (without the initial 0) and the number.

You can make domestic and international calls from public phones at the post office or phone boxes on the street. These accept credit cards or telephone

---

Smoking
From July 2009 it became an offence to smoke in any enclosed space. Smoking is also forbidden on all forms of public transport.

---

cards (*telekart*) which can be bought at the post office or some newsstands and kiosks.

Mobile phones: Turkey is on the GSM mobile network (North American visitors will need a tri-band phone). Buying a pay-as-you-go SIM card is a straightforward procedure which can be done at the airport. The domestic suppliers are Türkcell, Vodafone and Avea.

TIME
Turkey is on GMT plus two hours (plus three hours in summer), making it two hours ahead of the UK all year round. Turkish clocks go forward on the last Sunday in March and back on the last Sunday of October.

TIPPING
It's usual to round a taxi fare to the nearest lira and

leave 10 to 15 per cent for waiters in restaurants (round up to the nearest convenient whole number). Hamam staff are usually most emphatic about their apparently now traditional right to a 10 per cent tip.

TOURIST INFORMATION
The main tourist office is in Sultanahmet Park, close to the tram stop (tel: 0212-518 1802).
Turkish tourist offices abroad:
UK: 4th Floor, 29-30 St James's Street, London SW1A 1HB; tel: 020-7839 7778; www.goturkey.com
US: 821 UN Plaza, New Yirk NY 10017; tel: 212 687 2194/5. www.tourismturkey.org

VISA INFORMATION
Most nationalities (but not New Zealanders) require a visa which can be bought at the airport or land border on arrival and usually lasts for three months. Fees vary according to nationality and must be paid in foreign currency. At the airport you should join the queue for a visa *before* proceeding to the immigration desks.

45

Fashion

Many Turks are very fashion conscious and consequently the city is not short of shops featuring all the big international brand names, often in or near the four and five-star hotels. Of the two most famous designers with Turkish names, Rifat Özbek was born in İstanbul but studied in London, while Hüseyin Çağlayan was born in Turkish Cyprus and also studied in London. Recently, however, a younger generation of designers is starting to make its mark. Check out the small boutiques of Serdar-ı Ekrem Caddesi and Camekan Sokak in Galata to get an idea. *See also Bazaars and Shopping, p.32.*

Started in 2009, **İstanbul Fashion Week** looks set to become a regular fixture in the city's calendar although a firm date is yet to be established. In 2010 it took place in **February. Better established is Galatamoda**, a showcase for younger designers which takes place around the Galata Tower every May.

BARGAINS, OUTLETS & SECOND-HAND STORES

In general the Turks look down on the idea of anything second-hand, which means that there are no trendy charity shops where you can throw together a chic new image for a handful of lira.

Berrin Akyüz

Akarsu Yokuşu Sokak 22, Cihangir; tel: 0212-251 4125; Mon–Sat 10am–7pm; funicular: Taksim; map p.117 C3
This is a rare but extremely popular vintage clothing shop – search hard though for the exact item you are looking for – set in a trendy part of town.

Binbavul Vintage

Galipdede Caddesi 66, Galata; tel: 0212-243 7218; Mon–Sat 10am–6pm; funicular: Tünel; map p.116 B2
This is a giant rummage sale set in a warehouse full of all sorts of second-hand clothes and shoes that will need a lot of sifting through to find that perfect bargain.

Olivium Outlet Centre

Prof Dr Muammer Aksoy Caddesi 1/1, Zeytinburu; tel: 0212-547 7453; daily 10am–10pm; bus: 93 from Eminönü to Adliye
Four-floor shopping mall completely devoted to outlet stores for well-known labels such as Benetton, Diesel, Levi's and Mavi Jeans.

BOUTIQUES

Bahar Korçan

Serdar-ı Ekrem Caddesi 9, Galata; tel: 0212-243 7320; Mon–Sat 10am–7pm, Sun noon–7pm; funicular: Tünel; map p.116 B2
Exquisitely crafted dresses, lingerie and nightgowns all decorated with a discreet set of signature wings.

Above: İstanbul's shops offer many stylish accessories.

Gönül Paksöy

Atiye Sokak 6/A, Nişantaşı; tel: 0212-261 9081; Mon noon–7pm, Tue–Sat 10am–7pm; Metro: Osmanbey
This is a name to conjure with, Gönül Paksöy designs everything in the shop from delicate silks in muted colours to exquisite jewellery.

Lal

Camekan Sokak 4C, Galata; tel: 0212-293 2571; www.lallstan bul.com; Mon–Sat 10am–6pm; funicular: Tünel; map p.116 B2
An excellent range of T-shirts whose slogans and

Left: the city is developing a name as a fashion destination on the up.

works of Stella McCartney, Alexander Wang and others, and with a very see-and-be-seen brasserie on the ground floor.
SEE ALSO RESTAURANTS, P.103

Vakko
Abdi İpekçi Caddesi 33, Nişantaşı; tel: 0212-219 9660; Mon–Sat 10am–6pm; Metro: Osmanbey
Turkey's own home-grown luxury goods label stocking delicious silk scarves and ties as well as a wide range of fabrics.

motifs leave those in the Grand Bazaar standing. There is also jewellery made out of *oya*, the embroidery women used to make to edge their headscarves.

Midnight Express
Küçük Bebek Caddesi 7A, Bebek; tel: 0212-257 95 14, www.midnightexpress.com.tr; Mon–Sat 10am–6pm; bus: 25RE from Kabataş
Come here to shop for trendy local clothes designers such as Ümit Ünal and Zeynep Erdoğan as well as for pieces by jeweller Özlem Tuna.

Simay Bulbul
Serdar-ı Ekrem Caddesi, Sahkulu Bostan Sokak 22, Galata; tel: 0212-292 4586; www.sim-ay.com; Mon–Sat 10am–6pm; funicular: Tünel; map p.116 B2
The Grand Bazaar does the standard leather jackets, Simay Bulbul does the cutting-edge wedding dresses and evening-wear in paper-thin versions of the same fabric.

LABELS
Alexander McQueen
Abdi İpekçi Caddesi 21, Nişantaşı; tel: 0212-291 0754; Mon–Sat 10am–6pm; Metro: Osmanbey
All the extravagant frocks associated with the late lamented McQueen.

Beymen
Abdi İpekçi Caddesi 23/1, Nişantaşı; tel: 0212-373 4800; Mon–Sat 10am–8pm, Sun noon–8pm; Metro: Osmanbey
Cutting-edge department store showcasing the

Below: İstanbul's street fashions vary from edgy to traditionally conservative.

SHOES AND ACCESSORIES
Hotiç
İstiklal Caddesi 153, Beyoğlu; tel: 0212-245 4847; www.hotic.com.tr; Mon–Sat 10am–6pm; funicular: Tünel; map p.116 B3
Turkish chain shoe shop which manages some very appealing designs for men and women.

Lastik Pabuç
Camekan Sokak 4/H, Galata; tel: 0212-293 7923; www.lastikpabuc.com; Mon–Sat 10am–6pm; funicular: Tünel; map p.116 B2
Intriguing and original range of layered handbags and sun visors.

If all you want is a cheap T-shirt or woolly jumper to tide you through then you should hotfoot it across to Kadıköy on a Tuesday to browse the **Tarihi Salı Pazarı** (Historic Tuesday Market), a vast affair of almost limitless possibilities, now inconveniently relocated to Hasanpaşa which is accessible either by bus from beside the Fenerbahçe Stadium or by taxi.

Festivals

Istanbul has a wonderful range of annual festivals and events, some of them religious, some of them cultural and some of them just an excuse for a knees-up. The best known events are the International Film and Music festivals for which advance booking is almost always required, especially for popular events such as the annual rendering of Mozart's *Die Entführung aus dem Serail* staged inside the Topkapı Palace. Publicity for ad hoc events is usually poor to non-existent, and when it does happen is often only in Turkish. *Time Out İstanbul in English* will sometimes have the details.

JANUARY

New Year's Day

New Year (*Yılbaşı*) is becoming more popular. The focus is Taksim Square but the crowds can be large, and there are pickpockets. Luxury hotels offer special menus.

APRIL

İstanbul International Film Festival

Mid-April; www.iksv.org/film/ english lists venues
Independent films from around the world plus Turkish ones (not subtitled). Tickets sell quickly.

Tulip Festival

In mid-April millions of tulips bloom in the city's parks (including Gülhane

Above: introducing a screening at the Film Festival.

Park, Emirgan Woods and the grounds of the Khedive's Villa in Çubuklu); the precise date to celebrate varies from year to year.

St George's Day

23 April; St George's Monastery, Büyükada; ferry: Büyükada, then phaeton or long walk
Christians and Muslims ascend together to a hilltop monastery where a shepherd boy is said to have found a miraculous icon. As they go they unspool cotton reels and drape the thread on the

trees. Cubes of sugar are also handed out.
SEE ALSO WALKS AND VIEWS, P.111

MAY

Hidrellez

5-6 May; Çatladıkapı Park, Küçük Ayasofya; www.hidrellez. org; train: Kumkapı, then 20 minute walk; map p.121 C1
Balkan Gypsy spring music festival by the Sea of Marmara. Increasingly commercialised but still good fun. Write a wish on a piece of paper and hang it on a *nahıl* (wishing tree).

Chill Out Festival

Late May; Kemer Golf and Country Club; tel: 0212-283 5050; www.chilloutfest.com
Sunday rock festival attracting local and international acts.

Anniversary of Conquest of Constantinople

29 May
Prayers at the tomb of Mehmed II behind Fatih Mosque, reenactments in front of Belgradkapı and fireworks in Balat.

Left: celebrating the end of Ramadan.

One of the most important of all Islamic celebrations, **Ramadan** (*Ramazan* in Turkish) is a month of fasting from dawn to dusk on dates set according to the lunar calendar which moves forward by eleven days each year. After *iftar*, the end-of-fast meal, Beyazıt Square is a focus of the celebrations with more low-key festivities in Gazi Park in Taksim.

SEPTEMBER

İstanbul Biennal

Biennial arts extravaganza, next due in 2011 in a wide variety of venues all around the city.

OCTOBER

Akbank Jazz Festival

Third week of October; tel: 0212-252 3500; www.akbank-sanat.com

Jazz artists descend on İstanbul for concerts staged in the Akbank Art Gallery on İstilal Caddesi, CRR, Babylon, Roxy, Ghetto and Aya İrini.

Filmekimi film festival

Mid-October; Emek Cinema; İstiklal Caddesi, Yeşilcam Sokak 5; tel: 0212-293 8439; map p.116 B3

Opportunity to preview award-winning films from around the world before general release.

NOVEMBER

Anniversary of Atatürk's death

10 November

The anniversary of Atatürk's death at the Dolmabahçe Palace in 1938 is commemorated by a countrywide minute's silence on the stroke of 9.05 am.

JUNE

International İstanbul Music Festival

3-30 June; www.iksv.org/muzik/english lists all venues

Classical music with the Church of Aya İrini in the grounds of Topkapı Palace as the main venue.

Efes Pilsen One Love Festival

Mid-June; tel: 0212-212-3460; www.efespilsenonelove.com

Two-day rock and pop festival with local and international bands. Venues change annually.

JULY

International İstanbul Jazz Festival

1-20 July; www.iksv.org lists all venues

A broad-based jazz event in a variety of locations across the city.

AUGUST

Altın Eller (Golden Hands) Festival

Mid-August, Taksim Gazi Park; funicular: Taksim; map p.117 C4

Craftsmen and women from all over Turkey set up stalls in this park.

Below: the Formula One race is a major event *(see Sport, p.104)*.

Food and Drink

Turkish cookery – at its best – can be counted among the greatest in the world. Eating out is a passion here and you can hardly move in the city for restaurants to suit a wide range of budgets. Of course some meals are better than others but the excellent quality of the fruit, vegetables and meat on offer in the markets guarantees that a really bad dinner will be a rarity. As elsewhere, you'll pay more for plush surroundings and great views, but the real budget-buster tends to be alcohol, hammered here with sin taxes. *See also Bars and Cafés, p.28, and Restaurants, p.98.*

TURKISH CUISINE

STARTERS

The Turks are keen drinkers of soup (*çorba*), whether on its own for breakfast or as a starter to a full meal. Probably the most popular soup is lentil (*mercimek*) but you'll also find yoghurt soup (*yoğurt çorbası*), tomato soup (*domates çorbası*) and even tripe soup (*işkembe çorbası*) - an esteemed hangover cure - on the menu.

But the most popular starters are usually *mezes*,

Below: stuffed peppers make a great vegetarian option.

an assortment of small hot and cold dishes that are the Turkish take on tapas and best sampled when there are a few of you to share. Typical hot mezes include *sigara börek (*tubular pastries filled with cheese and parsley), *Arnavut ciğeri* (Albanian liver), *fırında mantar* (mushrooms stuffed with melted cheese) and *kalamar* (calamari). Cold mezes include *ahtapot salatası* (octopus salad), *cacık* (yoghurt flavored with garlic, cucumber, mint and dill), *fava* (mashed broad beans), *haydari* (yoghurt mixed with aubergine and garlic) and *Antep ezmesi* (tomato, red pepper and walnut salad).

MAINS

Turkey's gift to the rest of the world has been the *döner kebap* (lamb grilled on an upright spit and thinly spliced) but in İstanbul you may want to try *İskender kebap*, the delicious variation that comes on a bed of soft

Forget the idea of a crystal ball. In İstanbul if you want to know what the future holds you need someone skilled in *fal*, the ancient art of reading coffee grains. Since this is frowned on by the authorities, readings are often 'free' while the coffee is more expensive than usual. Expect the usual guff about handsome strangers and unforeseen fortunes. There are lots of *fal*-offering cafés in and around İstiklal Caddesi in Beyoğlu.

bread with a dollop of yoghurt beside it. Other staple main dishes include *şiş kebap* (chunks of lamb grilled on a skewer), *tavuk şiş* (the same but with chicken) and *Adana kebap* (spicy pats of meat baked on a skewer).

Kebabs not your thing? Then why not try *köfte*, tender meatballs usually served with half a loaf of bread and a helping of *piyaz* (white beans). *Ciğ köfte* is an uncooked variety, best sampled only in winter. Vegetarians should

Left: preparing fast food at an outdoor kitchen.

look for *etsiz ciğ köfte* (meatless uncooked 'meatballs') which can be surprisingly tasty.

DESSERTS

Turks love sweets so much that there were once whole pudding shops devoted to milk puddings, amongst which *sütlaç* (rice pudding) is king. These are now undergoing a renaissance and branches of Özsüt serve a range of milk puddings including *keşkül* (milk and almond powder pudding sprinkled with ground almonds and pistachios), *tavukgöğsü* (sweet milk pudding mixed with puréed chicken breast), *kazandibi* (*tavukgöğsü* with a caramelized crust) and *supangle* (chocolate mousse with choux pastry in the middle).

More readily available is the famous layered filo pastry and nut dessert soaked in syrup, *baklava*. *Künefe* is a delicious alternative made of hot melted cheese topped with a type of sweet 'shredded wheat'.

STREET FOOD

Hygiene regulations may be slowly killing off İstanbul's street food but for the time being you can still grab a breakfast *simit* (ring-shaped sesame-seed-topped bun) along with the locals. For lunch few things beat a quick *balık ekmek arası* (fish sandwich) bought from one of the floating kitchens at Eminönü. In the Fish Market off İstiklal Caddesi you can also snap up a quick *midye tava* (fried mussels); *midye dolması* (mussels stuffed with rice, raisins and pine kernels) are on sale on street corners.

ALCOHOL

Islam may frown on alcohol but Turkey's mixed heritage means that there has always been a strong wine-drinking tradition here. Until recently Turkish wine was a very hit or miss commodity but recently quality has been improving steadily. *Rakı,* the aniseed drink known as 'lion's milk', is the tipple of choice with many men who dilute it to taste with water and accompany it with chickpea nibbles or perhaps some fruit. Efes Pilsen is the most readily available beer. Hotels and upmarket restaurants also stock a range of imported drinks although the prices are pretty eye-watering. Don't expect to find alcohol available in the small, simple local restaurants called *lokantas* though.

FOREIGN FOOD

İstanbul is one of the few places in Turkey where it's

Below: Turkish sweets include the famed 'delight' and baklava.

Turkish coffee may be world-famous but in reality it's *çay* (tea) that oils the wheels of daily life here. Drunk in small tulip-shaped glasses it's surprisingly refreshing even in the heat. Ask for it *açık* to avoid a full-on caffeine assault.

But Turkish coffee is also staging a comeback as an after-dinner drink. Served in tiny porcelain cups, it's thick and strong, and comes with a dense layer of grains at the bottom. Ask for it *sade* (sugar-free), *az şekerli* (with a little sugar), *orta şekerli* (with a little more sugar) or *çok şekerli* (with lots of sugar).

Above: the ubiquitous glasses of tea that are served everywhere.

possible to find a range of foreign cuisines – everything from Chinese, Japanese and Korean to French, Italian and Russian. If you're only here for a few days that may not matter to you, but long-stay visitors tend to tire of a relentless diet of kebabs. 'New Turkish' cookery is served at many better restaurants. It's a fusion cuisine mixing the best elements of local food with plunderings mainly from the Middle Eastern and Mediterranean kitchen.

Below: a popular souvenir, boxes are sold in the bazaars.

FOOD SHOPS

EMİNÖNÜ AND THE GOLDEN HORN

Ali Muhiddin Hacı Bekir
Hamidiye Caddesi 83, Eminönü; tel: 0212-522 0666; www.haci bekir.com.tr; Mon–Sat 8am–8pm; tram: Eminönü; map p.121 C3
The original Turkish delight (*lokum*) shop, in business since 1777 and still going strong. Ask them to pack you a mixed (*karışık*) box to make the most of the treat.

Kurukahveci Mehmet Efendi
Cnr Tahmis Sokak and Hasırcılar Caddesi, Tahtakale; tel: 0212-511 4262; www.mehmet efendi.com; Mon–Sat 9am–6.30pm; tram: Emin önü; map p.120 C3
This tiny cornershop just outside the Spice Market always has queues, its customers' noses twitching at the irresistible smell of roasting beans.

Namlı Şarküteri
Hasırcılar Caddesi 14-16, Tahtakale; tel: 0212-511 6393; tram: Eminönü; map p.120 C3
Fight your way past the

haunches of rust-red *pastırma* (pastrami) to drool over the luxurious offerings in this famous charcuterie which has a tasting café upstairs. There's a more spacious branch in Karaköy but it lacks the atmosphere of the congested original.

KARAKÖY, TOPHANE AND BEŞİKTAŞ

Karaköy Güllüoğlu
Rıhtım Caddesi, Karaköy; tel: 0212- 293 0910, www.kara koygulluoglu.com; tram: Karaköy; map p.116 B1
Huge selection of baklavas and similar pastries including varieties specially baked for diabetics and for vegetarians (using olive oil instead of animal fat).

BEYOĞLU

La Cave
Sıraselviler Caddesi, Cihangir; tel: 0212-243 2405; www. lacavesarap.com; daily 9am–9pm; funicular: Taksim, then 10-minute walk; map p.116 C3
Oenophile heaven with an enormous choice of wines from Turkey and all over the world.

Right: freshly-landed crab at the Kumkapı fish market.

Sütte

Duduodalar Sokak 12, Balıkpazarı, İstiklal Caddesi; tel: 0212-293 9292; funicular: Taksim, then 15-minute walk; map p.116 B3

Excellent and long-lived delicatessen inside the Fish Market where you can even find pork products occasionally.

FISH MARKETS

SULTANAHMET AND KUMKAPI

İstanbul's freshest fish market is on the shore at Kumkapı whence the fishing boats still set sail for the Sea of Marmara. Buy your own, or eat at one of the fish restaurants right beside it on the shore or just inland to take full advantage.

KARAKÖY, TOPHANE AND BEŞİKTAŞ

There's a small fish market right beside the Galata Bridge which must be very frustrating for its permanently resident fishermen who never seem to land anything bigger than a tiddler.

BEYOĞLU

Just off Istiklal Caddesi the Balık Pazarı (Fish Market) used to be more of an İstanbul institution than it is since a recent restoration stripped it of some of

> Day-to-day menu toppers include *levrek* (sea bass) and *çıpura* (sea bream). In winter the locals love *hamsi* (anchovies), as shipped from the Black Sea. *Kalkan* (turbot) is another popular seasonal (and pricy) choice.

its atmosphere. It's still a good place to get a feel for what costs what though.

FOOD MARKETS

The freshest fruit, vegetables and cheese are usually available at İstanbul's street markets which rotate around the city depending on the day of the week. The largest takes place in **Çarşamba** behind the Fatih Mosque every Wednesday, although the most convenient for visitors is the Wednesday market that sets up beside the Sphendone in Sultanahmet heading down from the Hippodrome towards Küçük Ayasofya.

SPICE MARKET

Mısır Çarşısı, Eminönü; Mon–Sat 8.30am–6.30pm, also Sun from mid-Jun to mid-Sept; tram: Eminönü; map p.120 C3

Visitors tend to shop inside the Spice Market while locals shop outside where there are some wonderful fruit and vegetable stalls, and a great choice of cheese, including interesting Turkish varieties such as *Edirne peyniri,* a creamy ewe's milk cheese, and *Van otlu peyniri,* which is studded with herbs, as well as the

> Most daily food shopping is done in neighbourhood *bakkals*, the equivalent of the old-fashioned cornershop and just as threatened now by the rise of the supermarkets. Most stay open all hours but stock a fairly limited range of staples such as tea, eggs, milk, cheese and tinned tomatoes. Of the big supermarket chains Carrefour tends to offer the greatest choice, with Migros and Tansaş bringing up the rear.

standard *kaşar*, a Cheddar-like cheese, and *beyaz peynir*, the soft white cheese that is used to stuff pastries.

Below: a great choice of seasonings at the Spice Market.

Gay and Lesbian

While homosexuality is not illegal in Turkey, it is not exactly popular either, although visiting gays are unlikely to encounter any problems. İstanbul is one of the few places in the country where there is an active gay scene, with a set of clubs and bars known for their same-sex preferences. A few hamams (Turkish baths) are also popular with a gay clientele although the authorities have closed some of the old favourites recently – discretion must be the watchword. As always, the big four and five-star hotels ask the fewest questions although there are also a few gay-friendly small hotels in the city as well.

INFORMATION

The best and most up-to-date source of information is the Gay & Lesbian section of the monthly *Time Out İstanbul in English* which keeps an eye on the fast-changing club scene.

ORGANISATIONS
Lambda
Tel Sokak 28/5, Beyoğlu; tel: 0212-245 7068; www.lambda İstanbul.org; daily 3–8pm; funicular: Taksim; map p.116 C3
The Turkish branch of the

Below: holding hands here is not taken to be a romantic sign, but one of friendship.

international Gay, Lesbian, Bisexual and Transgender Liberation Group, Lambda has been criticised for its low profile although perhaps that's not so surprising in light of recent government efforts to close it down.

BARS AND CLUBS

BEYOĞLU
Bigudi Café, Pub and Club
Balo Sokak 20/4-5, Galatasaray; tel: 0555-835 1822; www.bigudiproject.com; pub daily 2pm–2am, club Wed/Fri/Sat 10pm–5am; funicular: Taksim; map p.116 B3
İstanbul's only lesbian venue features a rooftop terrace club that is exclusively women-only. The pub below is open to gay men as well.

Club 17
İstiklal Caddesi, Zambak Sokak 17; daily 11pm–5am; funicular: Taksim; map p.116 C4
No frills, anything goes venue where those selling sex tend to congregate.

Hengame
Sahne Sokak 6/1, Balık Pazarı; tel: 0212-249 1178; daily midnight–4am; funicular: Taksim, then 15-minute walk; map p.116 B3
You might not think to stroll through a fish market in search of any action, but this is still the unlikely hangout of one of the city's foremost transgender bars.

Tek Yon
Sıraselviler Caddesi 63/1, Taksim; tel: 0535-233 0654; daily 10pm–4am; funicular: Taksim; map p.116 C3
Extremely popular venue that has recently moved upmarket and upgraded its décor. Two separate bars come paired with a garden for those still wedded to the weed.

Xlarge
Meşrutiyet Caddesi, Kallavi Sokak 12; tel: 0506-788 7372; www.xlargeclub.com; Wed–Sat 11pm–5am; funicular: Tünel; map p.116 B3
Vast and busy club housed in an ex-cinema that stages drag-show takes on

Left: Istanbul's gay scene is active but discretion is key.

Across the road from the Azapkapı Mosque and the Atatürk Bridge and easy to find, this hamam has been one of the few to escape the wrath of the authorities – so far.

BEYOĞLÜ

Aquarius

Sadri Alisik Sokak 29; tel: 0212-251 8925; daily 24hr; funicular: Taksim, then 15-minute walk; map. p.116 C3
It looks small from the outside but this sauna, advertising itself as 'the only gay sauna in İstanbul', actually manages to pack a swimming pool in as an extra.

HOTELS

BEYOĞLÜ

Eklektik Galata Evi

Kadribey Çıkmazı No. 4, Serdar-ı Ekrem Caddesi, Galata; tel: 0212-243 7446; www.ekle ktikgalata.com; funicular: Tünel; map.p.116 B2
Tucked away in a side street in an increasingly trendy part of town, this small guesthouse has seven colourful, individually designed bedrooms, most of them on the small side.

TRAVEL AGENCY

SULTANAHMET AND KUMKAPI

Pride Travel Agency

İncili Çavuş Sokak 33/11, Ateş Pasajı Kat 2, Sultanahmet; tel: 02132-527 0671; www.travela gencyturkey.com; daily 9am–6pm; tram: Sultanahmet; map p.121 D2
Gay-owned and operated agency specialising in catering for the requirements of same-sex couples and gay travellers.

A somewhat unexpected aspect of the İstanbul gay scene is the conspicuous presence of a large transvestite (*travesti* in Turkish) population, especially around Beyoğlu. Capitalising on this unexpected quirk, there is even a series of detective novels featuring a transvestite detective. Written by Mehmet Murat Somer, they kick off with *The Prophet Murders*, published in English in 2008.

famous pop icons as well as go-go dancing from 1am. Its never-ending bar is a sight to be seen. Straight folk also admitted.

CAFÉS

BEYOĞLÜ

Frappe

İstiklal Caddesi, Zambak Sokak 10A; tel: 0212-292 3834; www. frappeistanbul.com; daily 9m–2am; funicular: Taksim; map p.116 C4
If you'd rather enjoy a quiet meal than hit the dance floor, then this small café makes the perfect

choice, especially at weekends when a party atmosphere prevails. Feel free to stop by just for a coffee.

Inside Café & Lounge

Lamartin Caddesi 11/4, Talimhane; tel: 0212-235 7914; funicular: Taksim; map.p.117 C4
Excellent choice of international favourites such as pasta and pancakes at this relatively new but popular café in Talimhane, one of the city's suddenly trendy corners.

Sugar Club Café

İstiklal Caddesi, Sakasalım Çıkmazı 7; tel: 0212-245 0096; daily 11am–1pm; funicular: Taksim; map p.116 B3
Popular with foreigners and those in search of less high-profile encounters.

HAMAMS AND SAUNAS

KARAKÖY, TOPHANE AND BEŞİKTAŞ

Yeşildirek Hamamı

Tersane Caddesi 74, Azapkapı; daily 6am–9pm; tram: Karaköy, then 15-minute walk; map p.116 A1

55

Hamams and Spas

Something interesting has been happening to İstanbul's traditional *hamams* (Turkish baths). For decades they had been losing their clientele as private bathing facilities improved and their own looked shabbier and shabbier. A handful of bathhouses made a living out of tourists but on the whole the picture was poor. Then the four and five-star hotels started to open luxurious spa facilities often incorporating a modern *hamam*. Now suddenly Turkish baths are all the rage again and many historic baths dotted about the city have either been restored, are being restored or are for sale for huge amounts of money.

TRADITIONAL HAMAMS

SULTANAHMET AND KUMKAPI

Çağaloğlu
Yerebatan Caddesi 34; tel: 0212-522 2424; www.cagalog luhamami.com; daily 8am–10pm (women 8am–8pm); charge; tram: Sultanahmet, then 10-minute walk; map p.121 D2

The most famous of all the *hamams* not just for its beauty but also because its past rollcall of illustrious customers including Florence Nightingale, Franz Liszt and Rudolf Nuryev. Men and women bathe separately and men get by far the more impressive entrance. The masseuses are tip hungry; irritating given the admission price.

BEYAZIT AND FATİH

Çemberlitaş
Vezir Hanı Caddesi 8; tel: 0212-522 7974; www.cemberlitas hamami.com.tr; daily 6am–midnight; charge; tram: Çemberlitaş; map p.120 C2
If you've never been to a *hamam* before this is a

good place to start since prices are all-inclusive and the setting, inside domed chambers designed by Sinan, could hardly be bettered. The women's changing area has been renovated recently.

Gedikpaşa
Hamam Caddesi 65-7; tel: 0212-517 8956; www.gedik pasahamami.com; daily 6am–midnight; charge; tram: Beyazıt, then 10-minute walk; map p.120 C2
Restored in 2009, this *hamam*, dating back to 1475, is one of the city's oldest, and has men's and women's sections.

Süleymaniye
Mimar Sinan Caddesi 20; tel: 0212-519 5569; www.suley maniyehamami.com; daily 10am–10pm; charge; tram: Beyazıt, then 20-minute walk; map p.120 B3
This *hamam* was originally part of the *külliye* (complex) surrounding Sinan's magnificent Süleymaniye Mosque. Recently restored, it makes a gorgeous setting for a scrub although some people will be put off by the mixed bathing arrangements.

BEYOĞLU

Galatasaray
Turnacıbaşı Sokak 24; tel:

Below: hamams have been popular for centuries.

Built by Mimar Sinan in 1584

Çemberlitaş Hamamı
The Historical Turkish Bath

Left: the Cemberlitaş hamam is a mix of traditional and accessible; a good place to start.

By the time you read this the most wonderfully elaborate Ottoman *hamam* of all, the Haseki Hürrem Hamamı in Sultanahmet Square built by Sinan for Sultan Süleyman I's wife Roxelana in 1556, may have reopened to bathers.

0212-252 4242; www.galata sarayhamami.com; daily 8am–10pm (women 8am–8pm); charge; funicular: Taksim, then 15-minute walk; map p.116 C3
The men's section of this Galatasaray *hamam* is very beautiful. The women's, on the other hand, is cramped and unimpressive.

SPAS AND SHOPS

SULTANAHMET AND KUMKAPI

Ambassador Hotel
Ticarethane Sokak 19, Sultanahmet; tel: 0212-517 0002; www.hotelambassador.com; daily 8am–10pm; charge; tram: Sultanahmet; map p.121 D2
A delightful small spa with its own private *hamam* which you can have all to yourself by appointment. The massage treatments are highly recommended.

Jennifer's Hamam
Arasta Bazaar 135, Sultanahmet; tel: 0212-518 0648; daily 10am–8pm; tram: Sultanahmet, then 15-minute walk; map p.121 D1
A great range of hand-

woven towels, bath robes and textiles as well as Rosence products from Isparta, Turkey's rose capital.

BEYAZIT AND FATİH

Abdulla
Halıcılar Caddesi 62, Grand Bazaar; tel: 0212-527 3684; www.abdulla.com; Mon–Sat 9am–7pm; tram: Beyazıt; map p.120 C2
Bars of olive-oil soap, thick woollen *ehram* wraps from Erzurum and fine silk towels. Abdulla was the first of the new luxury shops in the Grand Bazaar and it is still a wonderful, if pricy, place to shop.

Language of the bathhouse
Kese, a mitt used to scrub bathers; *kurna,* the basins ringing the steam room; *göbektaşı,* the marble slab in the steam room for massages; *peştemal,* thin wraps used for going in and out of the bath; *havlu,* the thicker towels used for drying; *taş,* the bowls used to scoop water over yourself; *nalın,* sandals used inside the *hamam.*

KARAKÖY, TOPHANE AND BEŞİKTAŞ

Four Seasons İstanbul at the Bosphorus
Çırağan Caddesi 28, Beşiktaş; tel: 0212-381 4160; www. fourseasons.com/bosphorus; daily 9am–9pm; charge; bus: 25RE from Kabataş
Not the biggest spa but certainly one of the most luxurious. A couple can book the *hamam.*

Haremlique
Şair Nedim Bey Caddesi 1, Akaretler, Beşiktaş; tel: 0212-236 3843; Mon–Sat 9am–6pm; tram: Kabataş, then bus 25RE from Kabataş
Designed to evoke the Harem of Topkapı Palace, this shop has aromatic soaps, as well as luxurious bathrobes and *peştemals* (*hamam* towels).

THE BOSPHORUS

Caudalie Vinotherapie Spa
Les Ottomans Hotel, Muallim Naci Caddesi 68, Kuruçeşme; tel: 0212-359 1533; www. lesottomans.com; Mon–Fri 7am–10pm, Sat–Sun 8am–10pm; charge; bus: 25RE from Kabataş
The city's most unforgettably beautiful spa but extremely expensive, with lots of amazing treatments to indulge in.

History

c.680 BC
Megarians settle Chalcedon, modern Kadköy.

c.660
Megarians under Byzas settle Sarayburnu (Seraglio Point) which goes on to become the heart of old İstanbul.

AD64
Byzantium becomes part of the Roman Empire.

258
Gothic invaders destroy Chalcedon.

330
Emperor Constantine the Great crowns Byzantium the capital of the Roman Empire as Constantinople.

391
Christianity becomes state religion.

395
Death of Emperor Theodosius heralds final split between Eastern and Western parts of Roman Empire.

532–7
Emperor Justinian rebuilds Aya Sofya after it was destroyed in Nika Riots.

1204
Fourth Crusade descends on and sacks Constantinople.

1261
Byzantine government restored after period of Latin rule.

1453
Sultan Mehmed II ('the Conqueror') captures Constantinople for the Ottomans on 29 May.

1517
İstanbul becomes centre of Islamic Caliphate under Sultan Selim I.

1520
Sultan Süleyman the Magnificent ascends the throne. Start of Ottoman Golden Age.

1571
The Ottoman navy is defeated at Battle of Lepanto.

1709–30
Tulip Age under Sultan Ahmed III. Brought to an end by Patrona Halil Revolt.

1826
Sultan Mahmud II disbands the Janissaries and creates a modern standing army.

1839
The Gülhane Decree kicks off the Tanzımat period of reform.

1856
Sultan abandons Topkapı Palace for the newly built Dolmabahçe Palace in an attempt to westernise the city.

1876
Sultan Abdülhamid II declares, then abolishes a constitutional monarchy.

1908
Sultan Abdülhamid II declares second constitutional monarchy.

1914–8

Ottomans enter First World War on side of Austria-Hungary and Germany.

1919–23

Turkish War of Independence under leadership of Mustafa Kemal Atatürk. İstanbul occupied by British and French troops.

1922

Sultanate abolished, bringing to an end 469 years of rule by the same dynasty.

1923

Treaty of Lausanne ends war. Capital moved to Ankara. Republic founded on 29 October.

1928

Turkish alphabet switched from Arabic to Latin. İstanbul becomes city's official name.

1938

Atatürk dies in Dolmabahçe Palace on 10 November. İsmet İnönü becomes president.

1939–45

Turkey stays neutral during Second World War.

1950

First democratic elections won by Democrat Party under Adnan Menderes.

1960

Military coup leads to hanging of Adnan Menderes. İsmet İnönü becomes prime minister.

1965

Justice Party wins elections. Süleyman Demirel becomes prime minister.

1971

Second coup leads to a series of figurehead leaders whose policies are dictated by the military.

1973

First Bosphorus bridge opens.

1974–80

Political tension and street fighting ends in third military coup. Kenan Evren becomes president.

1983

Motherland Party wins elections. Prime minister Turgut Özal launches programme of economic reforms.

1988

Opening of second Bosphorus bridge

1993

Death of Özal heralds decade of weak coalition governments.

1997

'Post-modern coup' sees off Islamic government of Necmettin Erbakan.

1999

Two serious earthquakes devastate northeastern Turkey and parts of İstanbul.

2001

Turkish economy collapses following national banking crisis.

2002

Justice & Development Party (AKP) wins elections. Ex-İstanbul mayor Recep Tayyıp Erdoğan becomes prime minister. Start of period of rapid growth and development in Turkey, especially İstanbul's infrastructure.

2010

İstanbul is European City of Culture. Prime Minister Recep Tayyıp Erdoğan wins a controversial referendum to change the constitution. Route of third Bosphorus Bridge from Garipçe to Poyrazköy announced.

Hotels

The last few years have seen a flurry of building work that has seen the number of hotels in İstanbul rise dramatically. You can take your pick from a wide range of options, everything from five-star luxury in converted palaces and prisons to bargain-basement comfort in a boutique hostel. In between there is a wide range of excellent mid-priced hotels, especially in Sultanahmet, often with spectacular views of the Sea of Marmara and within easy walking distance of the city's main attractions. It goes without saying that all the chain hotels familiar to business travellers are well represented as well.

SULTANAHMET AND KUMKAPI

Adamar Hotel

Yerebatan Caddesi 47, Sultanahmet; tel: 0212-511 1936; www.adamarhotel.com; tram: Sultanahmet; €€; map p.121 D2

Beautifully renovated apartment block with 25 colourful and stylish rooms. In a city where views are ten a penny, this hotel still boasts a particularly spectacular one from its terrace-restaurant that seems to encompass most of the old city. It's handy for the Yerebatan Cistern and the Çağaloğlu Hamam.

Ayasofya Konakları

Soğukçeşme Sokak, Sultanahmet; tel: 0212-513 3660; www.ayasofyapensions.com; tram:

Above: Adamar Hotel offers fabulous views.

Sultanahmet; €€€ ; map p.121 D2

Get a real feel for Ottoman living in this complete cobbled street of pastel-coloured wooden houses converted into a hotel that was one of the city's first serious attempts at historic restoration. Each of the houses contains several rooms furnished with antiques, the best of them so close to Aya Sofya that you almost feel you could touch it. Two restaurants, a

café and a library complete the offerings.

Cheers Hostel

Zeynep Sultan Camii Sokak 21, Sultanahmet; tel: 0212-526 0200; www.cheershostel.com; tram: Sultanahmet; €; map p.121 D3

A new development in 2010 was the arrival of the city's first boutique hostel, housed in a an old house behind the Zeynep Sultan Mosque. Standards of space, décor and cleanliness are a cut above what you normally expect in a hostel – but the real winning asset is a rooftop bar with views of Aya Sofya to die for.

Empress Zoe Hotel

Akbıyık Caddesi 4/1, Sultanahmet; tel: 0212-518 2504; www.emzoe.com; tram: Sultanahmet; €€; map p.121 D2

American-owned and hugely popular boutique hotel with a range of rooms dotted around a pretty, secluded garden against the walls of an old Turkish bath. Some rooms

Price categories are for a standard double room including breakfast in the high season.
€ = below €75
€€ = €75-120
€€€ = €120-200
€€€€ = over €200

Left: the Four Seasons Sultanahmet.

and a great location overlooking the Blue Mosque make the Ararat a good deal for someone on a tighter budget. The terrace breakfast room could hardly have a better view.

Hotel Kybele

Yerebatan Caddesi 35, Sultanahmet; tel: 0212-511 7766; www.kybelehotel.com; tram: Sultanahmet; €€; map p.121 D2
Famous for its thousands of hanging glass lamps that even infiltrate the bedrooms, the Kybele, created out of a pair of townhouses, is a splash of colour both inside and out. Breakfasts are great and there's a small pavement café for passing the time of day with the owners.

İbrahim Paşa Oteli

Terzihane Sokak 5, Sultanahmet; tel: 0212-518 0394; www.ibrahimpasha.com; tram: Sultanahmet; €€€; map p.121 C1
Mere steps away from the Hippodrome, the 16-room İbrahim Paşa is a stylishly modern hotel where a roaring fire in the lobby sets the tone in winter. Rooms are on the small side – for most space opt for one of the newer ones. The breakfast room has the feel of a Parisian bistro about it.

Mavi Ev (Blue House)

Dalbastı Sokak 14, Sultanahmet; tel: 0212-638 9010; www.bluehouse.com.tr; tram: Sultanahmet; €€€; map p.121 D1
Just across the road from the Blue Mosque, the 27-room Mavi Ev is an unmissable blue-painted wooden building with rooms that hover midway

---

The days when you could stay in İstanbul for a song are long gone and prices have been rising rapidly as hotels upgraded their facilities to snare a better-heeled clientele. Those on the tightest budgets will be thrown back on the hostels of which there are a growing number, mostly concentrated in Sultanahmet but with a few over in Beyoğlu as well.

---

are teensy, but the Garden Suites are spacious and feature their own *hamams*. A spiral staircase to some rooms might not suit everyone.

Four Seasons Sultanahmet

Tevkifhane Sokak 1, Sultanahmet; tel: 0212-638 8200; www.fourseasons.com; tram: Sultanahmet; €€€€ ; map p.121 D2
Hard to believe it was, until the 1980s, a prison, but the 65-room Four Seasons Sultanahmet is now the essence of comfort and luxury just minutes away Topkapı Palace and Aya Sofya. Its restaurant is

renowned for its cuisine, and the Sunday brunch is an epicurean delight. The building itself is a magnificent piece of late Ottoman architecture but the rooms go for more modern décor and every convenience.
SEE ALSO RESTAURANTS, P.99

Hotel Ararat

Torun Sokak 3, Sultanahmet; tel: 0212-516 0411; www.ararathotel.com; tram: Sultanahmet, then 15-minute walk; €€; map p.121 D1
Twelve smallish but individually decorated rooms

Below: the wonderful terrace at İbrahim Paşa Oteli.

between Ottoman style and modernity. The restaurant on the roof terrace makes a great place to wind up the day with spectacular views all around.

Nomade Hotel

Ticarethane Sokak 15, Sultanahmet; tel: 0212-511 1296; www.hotelnomade.com; tram: Sultanahmet; €€€; map p.121 D2

Tucked away in a side street, the 13-room Nomade is a cosy little hotel with a homely feel to it and rooms that go for jazzy splashes of colour. The breakfast terrace may not be large but offers yet more splendid views, while the lobby lounge makes an extremely comfortable place to relax with a drink. The owners are women, so the Nomade has long had a reputation as a refuge for lone women travellers.

Ottoman Hotel Imperial

Caferiye Sokak 6/1, Sultanahmet; tel: 0212-513 6151; www.ottomanhotelimperial.com; tram: Sultanahmet; €€€; map p.121 D2

What was once a grungy hostel has been turned into a superb 49-room hotel separated from Aya Sofya by nothing more than a narrow cobbled street. The supremely comfortable rooms are decorated in fusion style with Ottoman touches, but you won't spend much time on them, so lovely is the view over the roofs and chimneys of a local *medrese* (seminary) from the roof terrace.

Ottoman Hotel Park

Kadırga Liman Caddesi 85, Kadırga; tel: 0212-516 0211; www.ottomanhotelpark.com; train: Kumkapı, then 15-minute walk; €€€; map p.120 C1

For those who want to escape the crowds, the 38-room Ottoman Hotel Park might fit the bill nicely since although tourism is descending on Kadırga rapidly, for the time being this is still primarily a residential area with the hotel facing a local park. Rooms

are extremely modern and comfortable and the lovely marble fountain in the lobby sets the tone for a stylish hotel that is a little ahead of the game.

Sarı Konak

Mimar Mehmed Ağa Caddesi Nos.42–26, Sultanahmet; tel: 0212-638 6258; www.istanbulsarikonak.com; tram: Sultanahmet; €€€; map p.120 D1

Family-run 25-room hotel in a restored wooden house just 10 minutes' walk from the main attractions. Each room is individually decorated and more spacious than in some other nearby hotels. The house next door has been turned into a set of comfortable self-catering apartments. The view of the Sea of Marmara from the breakfast terrace is breathtaking.

Sirkeci Konak

Taya Hatun Sokak 5, Gülhane; tel: 0212-528 4344; www.sirkecikonak.com; tram: Gülhane; €€€; map p.121 D3

Award-winning 52-room hotel overlooking the walls of Gülhane Park and within easy walking distance of the main sites as well as the Eminönü ferry terminals. The rooms have been decorated with great attention to detail (underfloor heating in the bathrooms, for example), and the small basement pool is a big plus in summer. The breakfast spread is nothing short of spectacular.

Yeşil Ev (Green House)

Kabasakal Caddesi 5, Sultanahmet; tel: 0212-517 6785;

Left: the delightful Yeşil Ev has a peaceful location.

Right: afternoon tea at the Gazebo lounge in the Çirağan Palace is a treat.

www.İstanbulyesilev.com; tram: Sultanahmet; €€€; map p.121 D1
Another of those places where you can dream yourself back to Ottoman days, the 19-room Yeşil Ev is a careful reconstruction of an original wooden mansion which has been furnished in suitably period style as well. There's a lovely courtyard garden restaurant set around a fountain, and the attractive cobbled street in front is closed to traffic, making this a quiet choice just minutes away from the main attractions.

BEYAZIT AND FATİH
Kariye Oteli
Kariye Camii Sokak 18, Edirnekapı; tel: 0212-534 8414; www.kariyeotel.com; bus: 38E from Eminönü; €€€; map p.114 B3
Sometimes forgotten because it's a little off the beaten hotel track, the Kariye Oteli is right beside the Chora Church (Kariye Museum) in a neighbourhood of old wooden houses that still retains some

People on longer stays might want to rent an apartment rather than a hotel room in which case it's worth knowing about İstanbul Holiday Apartments (Galata Kulesi Sokak and Camekan Sokak, Galata; tel: 0212-251 8530; www.İstanbulholidayapartments.com; funicular: Tünel: map p.116 B1) which has several superb places available in Galata, Cihangir and Fındıklı, most of them with splendid Bosphorus views.

authenticity. The 19 rooms are furnished à la the Ottomans, and there is a renowned Ottoman restaurant (**Asitane**) in the rear courtyard.
SEE ALSO RESTAURANTS, P.100

EMİNÖNÜ AND THE GOLDEN HORN
Daphnis Hotel
Sadrazam Ali Paşa Caddesi 26, Fener; tel: 0212-531 4858; www.hoteldaphnis.com; bus: 99A from Eminönü; €€€; map p.115 D2
Another off-the-beaten-track offering is the 19-room Daphnis which was created out of a row of stone houses in Fener by a female architect. Rooms are light and high-ceilinged, if a little narrow, and retain some original decoration. Kozz is a decent restaurant facing the Golden Horn across the road on the ground floor.

KARAKÖY, TOPHANE AND BEŞİKTAŞ
Çirağan Palace Kempinski Hotel
Çirağan Caddesi 32, Beşiktaş; tel: 0212-326 4646; www.kempinski-İstanbul.com; bus: 25RE from Kabataş; €€€€
Ultimate luxury in a 313-room hotel right beside the Bosphorus which is, in part, a careful recon-

struction of a 19th-century palace. That certainly doesn't mean behind the times though, as the rooms have been equipped with all the latest in gadgetry such as centrally controlled lighting systems. The restaurants are renowned, the infinity pool looking onto the Bosphorus is a joy, and afternoon tea in the lounge is a (just about) affordable splurge.
SEE ALSO SPORT, P.105

Conrad Hotel
Barbaros Bulvarı, Yıldız Caddesi, Beşiktaş; tel: 0212-227 3000; www.conradhotels.com; bus: 25RE from Kabataş; €€€€
When President Obama stayed here in 2009 it put the seal on the popularity of this 599-room behemoth of a hotel in a location which, while not immediately appealing and rather remote from the sights, is certainly good for security. Three restaurants offer Italian, French and Turkish cuisine. The lovely Yıldız Park is just a stone's throw away.

Four Seasons İstanbul at the Bosphorus
Çirağan Caddesi 80, Beşiktaş; tel: 0212-381 4000; www.fourseasons.com; bus: 25RE from Kabataş; €€€€

63

When it opened in 2008 this 166-room hotel, partially housed in a 19th-century palace, certainly looked as if it would give the nearby Çırağan Palace Kempinski a run for its money. As at the Çırağan by far the best rooms are those in the relatively small palace part of the complex although you should expect every comfort and amenity throughout the hotel. There is, as you might expect, a lovely outdoor pool and several restaurants and cafés, as well as a sprawling, inviting lounge.

Tom Tom Suites

Boğazkesen Caddesi, Tomtom Kaptan Sokak 18, Tophane; tel: 0212-292 4949; www.tomtom-suites.com; tram: Tophane, then 20-minute walk; €€€€; map p.116 B2

This hotel was created out of what was once an Italian convent. Being small and stylish it offers only 20 comfortable suites, equipped with every mod con, as well as a pleasant rooftop restaurant, and a comfortable ground-floor library. İstiklal Caddesi is a mere 10 minutes' uphill walk away.

W Hotel

Süleyman Seba Caddesi 22, Akaretler, Beşiktaş; tel: 0212-357-9116; www.whotels.com; bus: 25RE from Kabataş; €€€€

They don't believe in doing things by halves at the 134-room W Hotel. Housed inside a minor historic monument of the 19th century which once accommodated workers from the nearby Dolmabahçe Palace, the hotel is, nevertheless, the last word in stylish modernity, just with a luxurious Ottoman twist in the form of giant candlesticks and fabrics that evoke the kaftans section of the Topkapı Palace.

No views or pool but a great restaurant and lounge area go a long way to make up.

Witt İstanbul Suites

Defterdar Yokuşu 26, Tophane; tel: 0212-393 7900; www.wittistanbul.com; tram: Tophane, then 10-minute walk; €€€€; map p.116 C2

A finalist in the 2009 Wallpaper New Hotels awards, the 17 Witt İstanbul Suites are decorated in soothingly muted tones perked up with the designer flair for style. Organic food is a big thing at breakfast. And this is a part of town that is definitely on the up.

BEYOĞLU

Ansen Suites

Meşrutiyet Caddesi 130, Tepebaşı; tel: 0212-245 8808; www.ansensuites.com; funicular: Tünel; €€€€; map p.116 B2

With a bistro-style restaurant on the ground floor, this delightful 10-room hotel was one of the first to opt for the increasingly

Right: hip and stylish decor at the Witt İstanbul Suites.

Right: hip and stylish decor at the Witt İstanbul Suites.

popular suites-only option. Its rooms go for a stripped-back, minimalist look with just a nod to the Japanese take on interior design.

Büyük Londra Oteli

Meşrutiyet Caddesi 117, Tepebaşı; tel: 0212-245 0670; www.londrahotel.net; funicular: Tünel; €€€; map p.116 B2
Something of a time capsule, this was one of the great hotels of the 19th century whose history is woven into the fabric of Beyoğlu and whose guestbook records the stays of the likes of Ernest Hemingway. Now that the Pera Palace has had a facelift the 54-room Büyük Londra is left holding the candle for shabby chic, its ground-floor lounge a veritable rummage box of antiques and curios. Some of the bedrooms have been renovated, others haven't.

Ceylan Intercontinental

Asker Ocağı Caddesi 1, Taksim; tel: 0212-368 4444; www.intercontinental.com.tr; funicular: Taksim, then 10-minute walk; €€€€; map p.117 D4
Your bog-standard, 387-room, five-star hotel if there is such a thing as bog-standard when it includes a Palm Court tea room, several restaurants and a spa to supplement the all-mod-cons rooms. There's even a bar sporting Turkey's finest selection of whiskies.

Galata Anemon Hotel

Cnr Galata Meydanı and Büyük Hendek Caddesi, Galata; tel: 0212-293 2343; www.anemon

hotels.com; funicular: Tünel, then 10-minute walk; €€€; map p.116 B2
A rarity in Beyoğlu, this 27-room hotel, housed inside an old mansion block, goes for the late Ottoman antique look in its bedrooms which still come equipped with every comfort the modern traveller expects. The roof-terrace breakfast room is extraordinary, so close to the Galata Tower that you feel as if might just topple over on you.

Pera Palace Hotel

Meşrutiyet Caddesi 90–100, Tepebaşı; tel: 0212-251 4560; www.perapalace.com; funicular: Tünel, then 10-minute walk; €€€€; map p.116 B3
One of the city's truly great hotels built to house the original passengers arriving from Paris on the Orient Express and where Agatha Christie penned her *Murder on the Orient Express*, the Pera Palace presides over a stunning

Price categories are for a standard double room including breakfast in the high season.
€ = below €75
€€ = €75-120
€€€ = €120-200
€€€€ = over €200

view of the Golden Horn. Closed for renovation for more than a year, it is due to reopen in late 2010 when it is assumed that it will have retained many of its original features but will have modernised the décor and added all the electrical gadgetry so essential these days.

Point Hotel

Topcu Caddesi 2, Talimhane; tel: 0212-313 5000; www.pointhotel.com; funicular: Taksim; €€€; map p.117 C3
In newly fashionable Talimhane and within spitting distance of Taksim Square, the 194-room Point Hotel is a cheerful, friendly place whose stylish rooms are made all the more appealing for having copies of images by Ara Güler, one of the city's greatest photographers, on the walls. The Udonya restaurant is as authentic a Japanese restaurant as you'll find in town.

Richmond Hotel

İstiklal Caddesi 227; tel: 0212-252 5460; www.richmondhotels.com.tr; funicular: Tünel; €€€; map p.116 B2
The only hotel right on frantically busy İstiklal Caddesi, the 104-room Richmond has comfortable if unexceptional rooms

65

that would not be suitable for the disabled because of a few stairs up to the reception. On the roof is a branch of **Leb-i Derya**, a super-fashionable and highly regarded fusion restaurant.
SEE ALSO RESTAURANTS, P.102

The Marmara
Taksim Square;
tel: 0212-251 4696; www.themarmaraİstanbul.com; funicular: Taksim; €€€€; map p.117 C4
A city landmark. the 387-room Marmara bestrides Taksim Square and keep-fit fanatics can be seen at all hours of the day and night exercising in its gym with windows looking out over the square. The sprawling reception area feels a little old-fashioned but most of the rooms have been given an over-haul to bring them up to today's expectations in terms of décor. The rooftop restaurant and bar offer matchless views of the city.

The Marmara Pera
Meşrutiyet Caddesi 117, Tepebaşı; tel: 0212-251 4646; www.themarmarahotels.com;

funicular: Tünel, then 10-minute walk; €€€€; map p.116 B2
This is the Marmara's 203-room 'little' sister, just down the road near the Pera Palace. It is altogether smaller and more intimate, although its rooftop restaurant, **Mikla**, regularly appears in lists of the city's best eateries. The rooftop may be small but it's a distinct plus in the heat of the Turkish summer.
SEE ALSO RESTAURANTS, P.102

NİŞANTAŞI, TEŞVİKİYE AND MAÇKA
Bentley Hotel
Halaskargazi Caddesi 75, Harbiye; tel: 0212-291 7730; www.bentley-hotel.com; Metro: Osmanbey; €€€
Just across the road from the Military Museum, the 47-room Bentley Hotel is a sleek modern hotel that combines cool muted colours with a faintly Japanese take on minimalist décor that works extremely well. Corner suites boast views of busy Halaskargazi Caddesi, and one of them even has an outdoor shower. There's a small restaurant perched over the lobby.

Left: a decorative detail at Les Ottomans.

Park Hyatt
Bronz Sokak 35, Teşvikiye; tel: 0212-315 1234; http://İstanbul.park.hyatt.com; taxi; €€€€
Housed in the grand Maçka Palace, an Art Deco mansion designed in 1922 by Giulio Mongeri, the Maçka Palace is luxurious, with one two-floor suite even having its own private entrance to the street. Spacious bedrooms come with wet rooms: think private *hamam* basins and walk-in showers. The bar boasts a wall full of wines to put many a cellar to shame.

Sofa Hotel
Teşvikiye Caddesi 123, Nişantaşı; tel: 0212-368 1818; www.thesofahotel.com; Metro: Osmanbey, then 15-minute walk; €€€
Super-stylish 82-room modern hotel, so discreet you can walk straight past the entrance without noticing it. The lobby is large, bright and colourful with an excellent library at one end and the well thought of Longtable restaurant concealing its quirky charms behind a door on the other.

THE BOSPHORUS
Les Ottomans
Muallim Naci Caddesi 68, Kuruçeşme; tel: 0212-359 1500; www.lesottomans.com; bus 25RE from Kabataş; €€€€
Small in terms of rooms (just 10 of them) but large in terms of what it has attempted, Les Ottomans is a reconstructed Bosphorus *yalı* (wooden waterside mansion) with just a handful of vast rooms, only a few of them actually overlooking the

Right: the Hotel Splendid Palace has been a desirable retreat for 100 years.

Bosphorus. The enormous ground-floor lounge is filled with light from the water, and the spa in the basement is probably the city's best.
SEE ALSO HAMAMS AND SPAS, P.57

Radisson Blu Bosphorus
Çırağan Caddesi 46, Ortaköy; tel: 0212-310 1500; www.radissonblu.com; bus 25RE from Kabataş; €€€€
Squashed into a small space on the Ortaköy waterfront, the 120-room Radisson is a delightful hotel whose nautical-themed bar looks straight out on the water. Bedrooms feature crisp white bed linen against polished wooden floors. The candle-lit spa is a great place in which to end your day.

Sumahan-on-the-Water
Kuleli Caddesi 51, Cengelköy; tel: 0216-422 8000; www.sumahan.com; bus: 15 from Üsküdar; €€€€
Housed inside a restored liquor factory right beside the Bosphorus, the Sumahan-on-the-Water is a 20-room boutique hotel with a set of attractive, light-filled rooms, some of them on two storeys, a small restaurant and an excellent library of books about Turkey. The hotel's

Price categories are for a standard double room including breakfast in the high season.
€ = below €75
€€ = €75-120
€€€ = €120-200
€€€€ = over €200

own private boat is available to run guests across the water to the Kabataş transport interchange.

GREATER İSTANBUL
Hilton Hotel
Cumhuriyet Caddesi, Elmadağ; tel: 0212-315 6000; www.İstanbul.hilton.com; funicular: Taksim, then taxi; €€€€
One of the city's older hotels (although the décor has long since been brought up to date), the 498-room Hilton has a priceless asset in such a built-up city in that it has its own outdoor swimming pool. A huge conference centre dictates that many of the guests here will be on business.

Hotel Splendid Palace
23 Nisan Caddesi 53, Büyükada; tel: 0216-382 6950; www.splendidhotel.com; ferry: Büyükada; €€€
Dating back to 1911, this 74-room hotel with its distinctive red window shutters is a piece of Princes' Islands history. An oasis for a little longer for those who prefer their accommodation characterful rather than contemporary.

Sheraton Ataköy
Sahilyolu, Ataköy; tel: 0212-560 8100; www.starwoodhotels.com/sheraton; train: Bakırköy, then taxi; €€€€
It may be housed inside a characterless high-rise building, but this 285-room Sheraton, right beside the Ataköy Marina, offers such splendid views from the bedrooms that it's hard even to notice the details of the spotless modern fixtures and fittings. The restaurants, too, are excellent including a branch of the local chain Cookbook with amazing decor.

67

Language

For most visitors Turkish is not an easy language to pick up mainly because the vocabulary derives in large part from Arabic and Farsi. Grammatically it is also bamboozling for English speakers because of the fact that the verb goes at the end of the sentence and carries a series of suffixes to represent tense and person. But if you can manage even half a dozen words of the language Turks will be very appreciative. Start with *teşekkür ederim* ('thank you') and see how you get on. And don't worry – most Turks who work in tourism speak excellent English as well as multiple other languages.

BASICS

Hello *Merhaba*
Good morning *Günaydın*
Good day *İyi günler*
Good evening *İyi akşamlar*
Goodbye *Hoşçakalın*
How are you? *Nasılsınız?*
Fine, thanks *İyiyim, teşekkürler*
Excuse me (attention) *Afer-dersiniz*
Excuse me (sorry) *Özür dilerim*
Yes/no *Evet/hayır*
Please *Lütfen*
Thank you *Teşekkür ederim*
You're welcome *Bir şey değil*
What is your name? *Adınız me?*
My name is... *Benim adım...*
Where are you from? *Ner-elisiniz?*
I'm from England/America ... *Ben İngiizim/ Amerikalıyim*
I like... *Seviyorum...*
I don't like *Sevmiyorum*

DAYS OF THE WEEK/ MONTHS/TIME

Monday *Pazartesi*
Tuesday *Salı*
Wednesday *Çarşamba*
Thursday *Perşembe*
Friday *Cuma*
Saturday *Cumatesi*
Sunday *Pazar*

January *Ocak*
February *Şubat*
March *Mart*
April *Nisan*
May *Mayıs*
June *Haziran*
July *Temmuz*
August *Ağustos*
September *Eylül*
October *Ekim*
November *Kasım*
December *Aralık*

Yesterday *Dün*
Today *Bugün*
Tomorrow *Yarın*

Below: buying a ticket.

EMERGENCIES

Help! *İmdat!*
Call a doctor/the police/an ambulance *Doktor/polis/ ambulans çağırınız*
I'm lost *Kayboldum*
Hospital *Hastane*
Pharmacist *Eczane*
Police station *Karakol*

HEALTH

I'm ill *Hastayım*
I'm allergic to... *...alerjim var.*
Antiseptic *Antiseptik*
Antibiotics *Antibiyotik*
Aspirin *Aspirin*
Contraceptives *Prezervatif*
Diarrhoea *İshali*
Headache *Başım ağrıyor*
Medicine *İlaç*
Morning after pill *Ertesi gün hapları*
Pregnant *Hamile*
Suncream *Güneş kremi*
Tampons *Tampon*

IN A RESTAURANT

Can I have the menu please? *Menüyü lütfen?*
The bill please *Hesap lüt-fen*
I don't eat meat *Hiç et yemiyorum*
I'd like... *... istiyorum*

Gülhane Parkı

Arkeoloji Müzesi
Yerebatan Sarnıcı

Topkapı Sarayı
Sahilyolu

Left: major tourist destinations are very well signposted.

Sixty *Altmış*
Seventy *Yetmiş*
Eighty *Seksen*
Ninety *Doksan*
One hundred *Yüz*
One thousand *Bin*

SHOPPING
Do you have...? ... *var mı?*
We don't have it *Yok*
What is this? *Bu ne?*
How much is this? *Ne kadar?/ kaç para?*
How much for each? *Tanesi ne kadar?*
It's too expensive *Pahalı*
Can I look at it? *Bakabilir miyim?*
Can I taste it? *Tadabilir miyim?*
Working hours *Çalısma saatleri*
Open *Açık*
Closed *Kapalı*

SIGHTSEEING
Where is...? *...nerede?*
Mosque *Camii*
Museum *Müze*
Palace *Saray*
Tourism office *Turizm Danısma Bürosu*
Entrance *Giriş*
Exit *Çıkış*

TRANSPORT
Bus *Otobüs*
Bus station *Otogar*
Ferry *Vapur/feribot*
Landing stage *İskele*
Ticket *Bilet*
Train *Tren*
Train station *Gar*
Tram *Tramvay*

USEFUL PHRASES
God willing *İnshallah*
Get well soon *Geçmiş olsun*
Slow down *Yavaş yavaş*
OK *Tamam*
No problem *Sorun yok*
It doesn't matter *Önemli değil*

Cheers! *Şerefe!*
Bon apetit! *Afiyet olsun!*
Knife *Bıcak*
Fork *Çatal*
Spoon *Kaşık*
Plate *Tabak*
Wine glass *Kadeh*
Where is the toilet? *Tuvalet nerede?*

LANGUAGE DIFFICULTIES
Do you speak English? *İngilizçe konuşuyor musunuz?*
I don't speak Turkish *Türkçe konuşmuyorum*
Could you repeat that? *Tekrar eder misiniz?*
I don't understand *Anlamıyorum/anlamadım*
I understand *Anlıyorum/anladım*
Please speak more slowly *Lütfen daha yavaş konuşunuz*
Please write it down *Lütfen yazarsınız*

NUMBERS
One *Bir*
Two *İki*
Three *Üç*
Four *Dört*
Five *Beş*

Turkish has several characters that are not in the Latin alphabet and which have their own particular pronunciation. Of the easier ones to get to grips with the 'ç' character is pronounced 'ch' and the 'ş' character is pronounced 'sh'. Visitors usually have more trouble with the dotless 'ı' which is pronounced 'uh', the 'ö' which is prnounced like the 'ur' in fur and the 'ü' which is pronounced like the 'ew' in few.

One of the most important things to be aware of is the Turkish 'c' which is pronounced like the English 'j' so that 'Camii (mosque)' is pronounced 'jami' and 'caddesi (street)' 'jaddesi'. The 'ğ' character is effectively silent.

Six *Altı*
Seven *Yedi*
Eight *Sekiz*
Nine *Dokuz*
Ten *On*
Eleven *Onbir*
Twelve *Oniki*
Twenty *Yirmi*
Thirty *Otuz*
Forty *Kırk*
Fifty *Elli*

69

Literature

In 2006 Turkish literature received a big shot in the arm when the İstanbul-born writer Orhan Pamuk won the Nobel Prize for Literature. Although relatively few Turks are regular readers, traditionally they have held writers, particularly poets, in considerable regard and the city is dotted with memorials to its authors. The sudden switch from use of the Arabic alphabet to the Latin alphabet in 1928 cut most of the population off from Ottoman Turkish literature. However, a growing number of modern Turkish novels and poems are being translated into English.

CONTEMPORARY TURKISH NOVELISTS

With the exception of *Snow* which was set in remote Kars, **Orhan Pamuk**'s books are inextricably bound up with life in İstanbul, and with the exception of *My Name Is Red* with modern İstanbul at that. Few of them make for easy reads although his stories of the goings-on amongst 16th-century calligraphers in *My Name Is Red* gave a new twist to the detective story. Roaring up behind Pamuk in the fame stakes comes **Elif Şafak** whose *The Bastard of İstanbul* saw her charged, like Pamuk before her, with 'insulting Turkishness'. Both authors were eventually acquitted and Şafak has gone on to pen *The Forty Rules of Love*, a remarkable retelling of the story of Celaleddin Rumi (Mevlana).

Tipped for the Nobel prize before Pamuk beat him to it was **Yaşar Kemal**, most of whose novels deal with life in the Çukurova region near Adana although a couple – *The Sea-Crossed Fishermen* and *The Birds are Also Gone* – are also set in İstanbul.

Other writers to look out for include **Buket Uzuner** whose most recent novel *İstanbullu* was set in the airport, and **Ayşe Kulin** whose *Farewell* has a backdrop of the British occupation of the city in 1923.

TURKISH POETS

The grand old man of Turkish poetry is **Nazım Hikmet** (1902–63) who spent much of his life in prison as a Communist and died in exile in Russia where he was buried. Other poets who have left their mark on the city include **Bedri**

> In İstanbul itself you will be able to pick up several descriptions of life in contemporary İstanbul and the rest of Turkey by expat writers. Most are published by Çitlembik and are available in all local bookshops.

Rahmi Eyüboğlu (1913–75) whose wonderful *Ballad of İstanbul* will win over even non-poetry-lovers; **Orhan Veli** (1914–50) whose statue looks out over the Bosphorus just before Rumeli Hisarı; and **Tevfik Fikret** (1867–1915) whose lovely house at Aşiyan, near Rumeli Hisarı, is open to the public.

TURKISH MEMOIRS

As well as his novels. Orhan Pamuk has written *İstanbul: Memoirs of a City*, an atmospheric evocation of the city of his youth. But for many the most poignant of all accounts of the city will be **İrfan Olga**'s heart-rending retelling of his family's collapse into poverty in the aftermath of the Turkish War of Independence in *Portrait of an İstanbul Family*.

FOREIGN WRITERS

A number of foreign writers have taken inspiration from the city. American Maureen Freely's novel *Enlightenment* looks at left-wing

Left: browsing at İstanbul's book market.

key *I Am Beautiful* concentrates on eastern Turkey.

Poets who have made the city their home include the American John Ash (*The Parthian Stones*). Also American, Paulann Petersen's poems touch on subjects such as the Four Seasons Hotel and a *nargile* café in *Blood Silk*.

BOOKSHOPS

BEYOĞLU

Homer Kitabevi
Yeniçarşl Caddesi 12A, Galatasaray; tel: 0212-249 5902; www.homerbooks.com; open Mon–Sat 10am–7.30pm, Sun 12.30–7.30pm; funicular: Taksim, then 15-minute walk; map p.116 B3

İstanbul Kitapçısı
İstiklal Caddesi 379; tel: 0212-292 7692; open Mon–Sat 10am–6.45pm, Sun noon–6.45pm; funicular: Tünel, then 10-minute walk; map p.116 B3

Pandora
Büyük Parmakkapı Sokak 8; tel: 0212-243 3503, www.pandora.com.tr; open Mon–Wed 10am–8pm, Thur–Sat 10am–9pm; Sun 1–8pm; funicular: Taksim; map p.116 C3

Robinson Crusoe
İstiklal Caddesi 379; tel: 0212-293 6968; open Mon–Sat 9am–9.30pm, Sun 10am–9.30pm; funicular: Tünel, then 10-minute walk; map p.116 B2

KADIKÖY AND ÜSKÜDAR
Greenhouse
Dumlupınar Sokak 17, Kadıköy; tel: 0216-449 3034; www.greenhousekitap.info; open Mon and Wed–Sat 10am–6.30pm; ferry: Kadıköy, then 15-minute walk

activism in 1970s İstanbul. The French traveller pen-named Pierre Loti (1850–1923) has a café named after him at Eyüp where he carried on the romance that inspired his novel *Ayizade (see p.29)*. British-born writers Barbara Nadel (whose books feature the chain-smoking Inspector İkmen) and Jason Goodwin (who created the eunuch investigator Yashim in *The Janissary Tree*) have set crime stories here. German-born but American-raised Jenny White has written a crime triology featuring a romance-minded magistrate called Kamil Pasha.

Foreign travel writers have written some memorable accounts of İstanbul, including *Innocents Abroad* by Mark Twain (1835-1910). Orhan Pamuk's favourite account of the city is the 19th-century Edmondo de Amicis' *Constantinople*. More recent accounts incluce Jeremy Seal's *A Fez of the Heart* and Tim Kelsey's *Dervish*. Finally, Brendan Shanahan's *In Tur-*

Below: Nobel Prize-winning author, Orhan Pamuk.

Monuments

Istanbul's attractions include palaces, mosques, museums and art galleries, as well as several other historic monuments dotted about the city that are not so easy to categorise. These vary from aqueducts dating back to Roman times and huge Byzantine water-storage cisterns to reminders of the Genoese trading colony in the shape of the Galata Tower and places like the picturesque Kamondo Steps in Karaköy. But perhaps the most conspicuous and yet often overlooked monument is the city walls that once ringed the whole of old İstanbul and in many places still survive in varying degrees of repair.

SULTANAHMET AND KUMKAPI

Basilica Cistern

Yerebatan Sarnıcı; Yerebatan Caddesi 13, Sultanahmet; tel: 0212-522 1259; www.yereba tan.com; daily Apr–Sep 9am–6-.30pm, 9am–5.30pm Oct–Mar; charge; tram: Sultanahmet; map p.121 D2

A water-storage depot might not sound like the most exciting of tourist attractions even if it does date back to Byzantine times but that's before you clap eyes on the Basilica Cistern (also known as the Yerebatan Sarnıçı or Sunken Basilica), a wonderfully romantic collection of 336 columns arranged in 12 rows with their bases submerged in water. Thirty or so years ago some genius in marketing came up with the idea of installing lights and a walkway so that visitors could explore the cistern. Stir in atmospheric music (often the *ney,* a flute especially associated with the whirling dervishes) and he'd come up with a recipe for an enthral-

ling and unusual attraction that is even better if you can manage to visit when a concert is being performed there. Crowds gather at the rear where a carved head of the Gorgon Medusa cannibalised from another site was reused as the base of a column; the fact that it is upside down is testimony to the fact that at the time (around AD532) no one was expected to view the cistern as anything other than a prosaic component of the water-distribution system.

Binbirdirek Cistern

Binbirddirek Sarnıcı; İmran Öktem Sokak 4, Sultanahmet; tel: 0212-518 1001; www.bin birdirek.com; Apr–Sep 9am–7pm, Oct–Mar 9am–6pm; charge; tram: Sultanahmet; map p.121 C2

The success of the Basilica Cistern encouraged the excavation of other cisterns in the city including the Binbirdirek, which means '1,001 Columns' in Turkish. It might be slighly disappointing, then, to find that there are only a paltry 224 columns here. Binbird-

Below: an ornate fountain at Topkapı Palace *(see box, right).*

Left: in the atmospheric Basilica Cistern.

Wherever you go in old İstanbul you will come across fountains *(çeşmes)* dating back to Ottoman times. These vary from the simple wall fountains that provided water for residents of each neighbourhood before piped supplies became available to huge ornamental structures, mostly dating back to the 18th century, such as the Sultan Ahmed III Fountain in front of the gateway into Topkapı Palace and the Tophane Fountain near the Nusretiye Mosque in Tophane.

irek has been drained of its water and serves as a concert venue-cum-restaurant that occasionally houses exhibitions as well. Although parts of it may date back to the reign of Constantine the Great (c.274–337), most of it appears to be of fifth or sixth century construction.

Caferağa Medresesi

Caferiye Sokak, Sultanahmet; tel: 0212-513 3601; daily 8.30am–7pm; free; tram: Sultanahmet; map p.121 D2

This tranquil little hideaway dates back to 1560 and originally housed the students of a seminary. It was designed by Sinan – whose bust adorns the courtyard – for Cafer Ağa, the Chief Black Eunuch at Topkapı Palace during the reign of Süleyman the Magnificent. What were once the students' cells now house craft workshops, while the attractive courtyard is home to a peaceful café.

Right: the Hippodrome is crowned by this Obelisk.

Goths Column

Gülhane Park, Sultanahmet; free; tram: Sultanahmet; map p.121 E3

At the Sarayburnu end of Gülhane Park, near the Setüstü tea gardens, stands this 15-metre-tall granite column which looks rather like the more famous Çemberlitaş Column in a much better state of repair. Apparently it was once topped with a statue of Byzas, the founder of

Byzantium. A battered inscription says that it was erected in memory of a victory over the Goths that may have been during the reign of Constantine the Great (c.274-337) or even earlier during the reign of Claudius II Gothicus (r. 268-70).

The Hippodrome

At Meydanı, Sultanahmet; free; tram: Sultanahmet; map p.121 C1

It may seem like nothing

In Ottoman times fountains were places where people collected their own water while *sebils* were staffed water dispensaries, often attached to mosques or on prominent street corners. Today old *sebils* have been converted to house small cafés, restaurants and kiosks. One even houses a small carpet shop.

more than a small park now but the Hippodrome once played a hugely important role in Byzantine life as the place where hugely popular chariot races were held. In the sixth century these races attracted the same sort of fanatical fans as some football teams do today, and in 532 the followers of the most important, the Blues and Greens, clashed so badly that Aya Sofya was burnt down along with two other nearby churches. Of its glory days little now remains bar one fine obelisk brought from Thebes in 392 by Emperor Theodosius II; another more battered obelisk probably erected by Constantine the Great or Theodosius I; and a piece of coiled metal that is all that remains of a bronze tripod adorned with three snakes' heads that seems to have been brought here from Delphi in Greece by Constantine the Great. The plinth of the main obelisk is especially interesting since it depicts scenes of the emperor bestowing laurels on a victorious charioteer.

Also in the Hippodrome is a large green-roofed fountain that commemorates the visit of Kaiser Wilhelm II to Sultan Abdühamid II in 1898.

Left: an Ottoman-era water fountain.

days but the battered, 35-metre-high Çemberlitaş Column is one of the few survivals from the reign of Constantine the Great when it formed the centerpiece of what was then the Forum of Constantine. Built to commemorate the emperor's decision to make Byzantium the capital of the Eastern Roman Empire, it was originally topped with a statue of the sun god Apollo. Today the column is held together with bands of metal, hence its names which means 'Hooped Stone' in Turkish.

Kıztaşı
Kıztaşı Caddesi, Fatih; free; bus: 38E from Eminönü; map p.119 E3

Reminscent of the Goths Column and Çemberlitaş Column, the Kıztaşı (Maid-

BEYAZIT AND FATİH
Aqueduct of Valens
Atatürk Bulvarı, Fatih; free; bus: 38E from Eminönü; map p.120 A3

An 18.5-metre-high double tier of arches, the Aqueduct of Valens is hard to miss since it straddles one of the city's busiest roads. Erected by the Emperor Valens in 375, it used to be a crucial link in the chain of structures that brought water from the wooded areas of Thrace into the city, a purpose it continued to serve into Ottoman times, hence its surprisingly good condition.

Çemberlitaş Column
Divan Yolu, Çemberlitaş; free; tram: Çemberlitaş; map p.120 C2

It may have seen better

en's Colum) was erected in the fifth century for the Emperor Marcian whose statue may once have stood on top of it. It takes its name from a carving of the Greek goddess of victory Niké that can be seen on the base.

EMİNÖNU AND THE GOLDEN HORN
Galata Bridge
Eminönü-Karaköy; free; tram: Eminönü/Karaköy; map p.121 C4
The Galata Bridge across the Golden Horn is one of those iconic sights of İstanbul that everybody sees at some point, even if only in passing. Perhaps surprisingly there was no permanent structure here until 1836 despite Leonardo da Vinci and others coming up with designs for a bridge centuries earlier. The model you see here today

is the fifth that has bridged the span and is famous for the fishermen who dangle their rods over its sides throughout the year. The fish restaurants on the underside make a great place to watch the sun set over the Süleymaniye Mosque. The much-pictured previous construction was dismantled and has now been re-erected as a footbridge linking Eyüp to Sütlüce at the far end of the Golden Horn.

> At the point where Divan Yolu leaves Sultanahmet Square stand the remains of a stone tower that was once part of the system for conveying water around the city. Beside it sits a stumpy monument that you might not even notice. This was once the Milion, the milestone from which all distances in the empire were measured.

KARAKÖY, TOPHANE AND BEŞİKTAŞ
Kamondo Steps
Bankalar (Voyvoda) Caddesi, Karaköy; free; tram: Karaköy, then 10-minute walk; map p.116 B1
A quirky one off, these curvaceously beautiful steps where provided by the wealthy Jewish banking family the Kamondos in the 1880s to provide a shortcut up to the area around Galata Tower.

BEYOĞLU
Casa Botter
İstiklal Caddesi 475–7; free; funicular: Tünel; map p.116 B3
İstanbul boasts a number of little-commented Art Nouveau buildings amongst which this is one of the gems despite its current neglected state. Decked out in carved stone roses and giant heads, it was designed by the Italian architect Raimondo d'Aronco in 1901 for a Dutchman named Jan Botter who was tailor to Sultan Abdülhamid II.

Çiçek Pasajı
İstiklal Caddesi, Galatasaray; free; funicular: Taksim, then nostalgic tram; map p.116 B3
Built on the site of a famous city theatre that burnt down in 1870, the Çiçek Pasajı was originally a development of shops and apartments called the Cite de Pera that became famous for the lively *meyhanes* (taverns) in its cobbled courtyard. It acquired its pretty name after they became the haunt of White Russian flower-sellers who had fled the Bolshevik Revolution and taken ref-

Left: the Galata Bridge is always lined with fishermen.

75

Above: some of İstanbul's remaining city walls.

uge in Turkey. Today this is still a pleasant place to spend a night out although restoration has robbed it of some of its atmosphere. For a livelier take on the *meyhane* scene you need to duck behind it into Nevizade Sokak.

SEE ALSO RESTAURANTS, P.102

Galata Mevlevihanesi

Galipdede Caddesi, Galata; charge; funicular: Tünel; map p.116 B2

If you want to watch an authentic performance of the famous whirling dervishes in İstanbul, few places can beat the lovely wooden-floored *semahane* (ritual hall) at Galata where women traditionally whirl with men (in 2010 the building was closed for restoration). Performances usually take place on a Sunday afternoon with precise times and dates posted on a board outside. At other times, the hall houses a small Museum of Court Literature with illuminated manuscripts and musical instruments.

Galata Tower

Galata Kulesi, Galata Meydanı, Galata; tel: 0212-293 8180; www.galatatower.com; daily 9am–8pm; charge; funicular: Tünel; map p.116 B2

An unmissable landmark on the city skyline, the Galata Tower (originally the Tower of Christ) with its witch's hat roof, is the last significant survival from the fortifications that used to surround the self-governing Genoese trading colony established here in the 14th century. Since then it has had a chequered history, used as a prison and lighthouse before being co-opted for a restaurant and nightclub. In 1648 it was also the setting for a ground-breaking endeavour when Hezarfen Ahmed Çelebi used it as a base from which to glide across

Below: the entrance to the Çiçek Pasajı.

to Üsküdar on a set of wings resembling an early hang-glider.

Republic Monument

Taksim Meydanı; free; funicular: Taksim; map p.117 C4

It's not as big as its renown might suggest but the monument in Taksim Square is as dear to the hearts of Turks as Nelson's Column is to those of the British since it commemorates the founding of the republic in 1923. Not surprisingly, heroic war leader Atatürk takes a prominent place in the decorative sculptures which were designed by the Italian sculptor Pietro Canonica in 1928.

THE BOSPHORUS
Anadolu Hisarı

Hisar Kale Sokak, Anadolu Hisarı; free; ferry: Anadolu Hisarı

Long before Sultan Mehmed the Conqueror succeeded in capturing Constantinople in 1453 the Ottomans had been eyeing up the prize, and Sultan Beyazıd I ('the Thunderbolt') had a castle built here at the narrowest point of the Bosphorus in 1398, ready for an assault on the city that ended in failure in 1402. The remains of Anadolu Hisarı (Asian Castle) are still fairly impressive although the 20th century saw a road carved right through the fortifications. You can only admire them from the outside.

Rumeli Hisarı

Bebek-Rumeli Hisarı Caddesi, Rumeli Hisarı; tel: 0212-263 5305; Thur–Tue 9am–noon &

12.30–4.30pm; charge; bus: 25RE from Kabataş

One of the great landmarks as you cruise along the Bosphorus is the huge fortress of Rumeli Hisarı (European Castle) just before the Fatih Sultan Mehmet Bridge. Built by Sultan Mehmed II in 1452 on land grudgingly ceded to him by the Emperor Constantine XI Dragases, the castle had three massive circular towers and many smaller ones. Unlike Anadolu Hisarı it served its purpose perfectly and within a year the sultan had seized the city. In 1953 the castle was completely restored to celebrate the 500th anniversary of the event. Today it's a pleasant place to while away a few hours and admire the Bosphorus views from the walls (although safety precautions are fairly minimal).

GREATER İSTANBUL
City Walls

As you drive into old İstanbul from the airport you can hardly fail to see the remains of the huge towers that once formed the land defences of Con-

stantinople. Dating back to the reign of the Emperor Theodosius II, these walls were repaired and rebuilt over the centuries and consisted of twin lines of fortifications with a moat in front of them.

Still today it's possible to walk the length of the land walls from Mermerkule (Marble Tower) on the Sea of Marmara to Ayvansaray on the Golden Horn where the land walls intersected with the rather less monumental sea walls. These continued all the way along the southern shore of the Golden Horn, round Sarayburnu (Seraglio Point) and then along the Sea of Marmara to rejoin the land walls at Mermerkule. Not much remains of the sea walls along the Golden Horn which have been largely lost to road-widening and housing, but as you drive along the busy Sahil Yolu (Coast Road) you will be able to admire the mighty remains of the Propontine sea walls that lined the Sea of Marmara.

SEE ALSO WALKS AND VIEWS, P.111

Right: the Rumeli Hisarı looms over the Bosphorus.

Mosques, Synagogues and Churches

Istanbul is full of mosques, every *mahalle* (neighbourhood) has its own mosque, sometimes with associated buildings such as fountains and schools that generally serve new purposes in the modern world. The Ottoman mosques are beautiful, awe-inspiring buildings, but you need to look much harder to find the city's finest churches and synagogues.

MOSQUES

SULTANAHMET AND KUMKAPI

Aya Sofya Museum
Church of Holy Wisdom, Aya Sofya Meydami, Sultanahmet; tel: 0212-522 0989; Tue–Sun 9am–7.30pm mid-June–mid-Sep, 9am–5pm mid-Sep-mid June; charge; tram: Sultanahmet; map p.121 D2
Is it a church? Is it a mosque? Is it a museum? Actually Aya Sofya has been all three things in turn, starting life as the great church of Emperor Justinian in 537, then becoming a mosque in 1453 after the Ottoman conquest of Constantinople, before being turned, finally, into a museum in 1935. Enormous but not especially beautiful from the outside which had to be buttressed in the 16th century against earthquake damage, the church-mosque is stunning once you step into the nave which is as large as and more spacious than St Paul's in London or St

Above: Chora Church is decorated with frescoes *(see p.82)*.

Peter's in Rome. The breathtaking space aside, Aya Sofya's greatest glory is a collection of Byzantine mosaics covered with whitewash in early Ottoman times and only revealed again in 1933 (one tiny seraphim only came to light in 2009). The finest of them are in the south gallery where a Byzantine Renaissance Deesis scene features almost photographic detail.
Behind Aya Sofya it is now possible to visit the tombs

of some of the 16th and 17th-century sultans via a separate entrance (admission free).

Küçük Aya Sofya Mosque
Küçük Aya Sofya Camii, Küçük Ayasofya Caddesi; tel: 0212-458 0776; train: Kumkapı, then 10-minute walk; map p.121 C1
Originally built by the Emperor Justinian in 527 as the Church of Sts Sergius and Bacchus, the newly restored Little Aya Sofya Mosque is a beautiful one-off with a two-tier

Left: the cascading domes of the Blue Mosque.

although it was originally designed to be entered from the Hippodrome.

BEYAZIT AND FATİH

Beyazıt Mosque

Beyazıt Camii, Yeniçeriler Caddesi, Beyazıt; tel: 0212-519 3644; tram: Beyazıt; map p.120 B2

Most people assume that Sinan's were the first of the great classical mosques of the early Ottoman period, but in fact the Beyazıt Mosque was erected between 1501 and 1506 by an architect about whom nothing is known except his name, Yakub Şah ibn Sultan Şah. Like the much younger Blue Mosque it is approached via a peaceful, shady courtyard with an ablutions fountain in the centre, and like the Blue Mosque it features a collection of domes, although only a measly two minarets, each of them attractively decorated with inlaid terracotta.

Fatih Mosque

Fatih Camii, Fevzi Paşa Caddesi, Fatih; bus: 31E from

circular portico surrounding what was once the nave. The friezes and capitals still retain their Greek inscriptions and Byzantine motifs. The courtyard and medrese added in 1500 offer craft workshops and a small café.

Sokollu Mehmed Paşa Mosque

Sokollu Mehmed Paşa Camii, Şehit Çeşmesi Sokak, Kadırga; tram: Sultanahmet, then 15-minute walk; map p.121 C1

This mosque is a delightful work of Sinan dating back to 1571 and carefully designed to fit into a steep hillside location, the Sokollu Mehmed Paşa Mosque contains one of the city's finest collections of İznik tiles, including many that incorporated the raised red glaze known as Armenian bole. The courtyard is completely ringed with a portico housing the cells of a *medrese* (seminary) whose lecture hall sits above the stairs leading up to the mosque.

Sultanahmet (Blue) Mosque

Sultanahmet Camii, Hippodrome; tel: 0212-518 1319; tram: Sultanahmet; map p.121 D1

With its matchless collection of six minarets, the Sultanahmet Mosque, the handiwork of Sedefkar Mehmed Ağa between 1609 and 1616, is a glorious tumble of grey domes and half-domes that clearly took some of its inspiration from Aya Sofya across the park via the intermediary of Sinan. This is the one mosque that almost all visitors to the city see, although many leave somewhat confused as to why it should be nicknamed 'the Blue Mosque' when there are other mosques so much more obviously that colour. Few, however, fail to be impressed by the sheer space beneath the dome which is supported by four so-called elephant's foot pillars. The most obvious way into the mosque is from opposite Aya Sofya,

Know your Mosque

Hünkar mahfili: private box for the sultan, often accessible via private entrance

Kürsü: seat from which imam reads Koran

Mimber: pulpit, usually at top of a flight of steps

Mihrab: niche in the wall facing towards Mecca

Minaret: tower from which call to prayer is made

Müezzin mahfili: private pew where muezzin sings responses to imam's prayers

Şadırvan: ablutions fountain

79

Above: İznik tiles at Sokollu Mehmed Paşa Mosque *(see p.79)*.

cially interesting because it still retains almost all of its surrounding *külliye* (complex) of social amenities including an *imaret* (soup kitchen), *caravanserai* (inn for travelling traders), several *medreses* (seminaries) and a *hastane* (hospital). Şuleyman the Magnificent and his wife Roxelana are buried in separate tombs to the rear, while Sinan himself is buried just outside the complex.

EMİNÖNÜ AND THE GOLDEN HORN

Eyüp Sultan Mosque
Eyüp Sultan Camii, Camii Kebir Sokak, Eyüp; ferry: Eyüp
This is the most sacred mosque in İstanbul, and for good reason. The Eyüp Sultan Mosque was built over the burial place of a companion of the Prophet Mohammed who had died during an Arab assault on the city between 674 and 678. It was completely rebuilt during the reign of Fatih Sultan Mehmed and became the place to which each new sultan would come to pray and be girded with the sword of Osman, the first sultan of the Ottoman dynasty, immediately after his coronation.

New Mosque
Yeni Camii, Yeni Camii Meydanı Sokak, Eminönü; tel: 0212-527 8505; tram: Eminönü; map p.121 C3
One of the last of the great imperial complexes, the New Mosque was completed in 1663 and originally stood right on the waterfront. The Spice Market originally existed to help defray its running

Eminönü; map p.119 D4
Approached from the main road the Fatih Camii, which stands on the site of the old Church of the Holy Apostles where many of the Byzantine emperors had been buried, looks more like a fortress than a mosque but that is because the actual mosque sat in the centre of a collection of associated buildings including several stout-walled *medreses* (seminaries). This was the first mosque built by Fatih Sultan Mehmed ('the Conqueror') who is buried in a fine tomb behind it.

Şehzade Mosque
Şehzade Camii (Mosque of the Crown Prince), Şehzadebaşı Caddesi, Fatih; tram: Laleli-Üniversite, then 10-minute walk; map p.120 A3

Built by Sinan between 1543 and 1548 to commemorate Süleyman the Magnificent's son Mehmed who had died of smallpox, this is one of the master architect's earliest works – and, some might argue, one his finest with its wonderfully decorated porticoed courtyard and twin mosques. Sadly, the tombs in the grounds are not open to the public – yet!
SEE ALSO RESTAURANTS, P.100

Süleymaniye Mosque
Süleymaniye Camii, Prof Sıddık Sami Onar Caddesi; tel: 0212-514 0139; tram: Beyazıt, then 10-minute walk; map p.120 B3
Built on top of the Third Hill of the old city and acknowledged as Sinan's masterpiece in İstanbul, the Süleymaniye was erected between 1550 and 1557, and is espe-

Mosques, Synagogues & Churches

Most of the city's mosques are open to visitors free of charge outside prayer times. Women should cover their heads, arms and legs; men, too, should be modestly dressed. Everyone should remove their shoes before entering. Donations are gratefully received and you may be given an official receipt.

costs. The brick-and-stone building attached to the side of the building was a suite of private rooms for the sultan; its recent restoration won prizes for its excellent quality which doesn't mean, however, that you'll be allowed inside it to see the results.

Rüstem Paşa Mosque

Rüstem Paşa Camii, Hasırcılar Caddesi, Tahtakale; tel: 0212-526 7350; tram: Eminönü; map p.120 C4

Everybody's favourite Sinan mosque, the tiny Rüstem Paşa built in 1560 on a platform above the Tahtakale bazaar is densely coated inside and out with İznik tiles which, as many people point out, give it a greater right to be

called a 'blue' mosque than the better known Sultanahmet (Blue) Mosque.

KARAKÖY, TOPHANE AND BEŞIKTAŞ

Dolmabahçe Mosque

Dolmabahçe Camii, Muallim Naci Caddesi, Dolmabahçe; tram: Kabataş; map p.117 D4

Large, light-filled and rather beautiful mosque right on the waterside designed by Nikoğos Balyan in 1853.

Kılıç Ali Paşa Mosque

Kılıç Ali Paşa Camii, Ali Paşa Mescid Sokak, Tophane; tram: Tophane; map p.116 C2

Another graceful work of Sinan designed in 1580 when he was in his nineties for Vice Admiral Kılıç ('The Sword') Ali Paşa, a hero of the Battle of Lepanto in 1571. Restoration work started in 2010 should see its equally antique *hamam* (Turkish bath) return to service soon.

NİŞANTAŞI, TEŞVİKİYE AND MAÇKA

Teşvikiye Mosque

Teşvikiye Camii, Teşvikiye Caddesi. Nişantaşı; Metro: Osman-

Above: at Beyazıt Mosque's abultions fountain *(see p.79)*.

bey, then 15-minute walk

High society mosque built in 1853 and boasting several 'target stones' in the courtyard.

THE BOSPHORUS

Ortaköy Mosque

Ortaköy Camii, İskele Caddesi, Ortaköy; bus: 25RE from Kabataş

Landmark mosque almost beneath the Bosphorus Bridge that was designed by Garabet Balyan in 1855. It's a virtual mirror image of the mosque at Dolmabahçe.

KADIKÖY AND ÜSKÜDAR

Atik Valide Sultan Mosque

Atik Valide Sultan Camii, Valide İmaret Sokak, Üsküdar; ferry: Üsküdar, then half-hour walk

This beautiful mosque with a peaceful courtyard forms the centerpiece of a complex of sadly neglected buildings designed by Sinan in 1583 for Nurbanu Sultan, the wife of Sultan Selim II. To find it stroll up Eski Toptaşı Caddesi (Old Cannonball Street) or take a taxi.

Below: the stunning Ortaköy Mosque on the Bosphorus.

Left: Ahrida Synagogue.

replacements for older churches that were destroyed by the mobs during the Nika Riots of 532. Sadly, you will only get to see its exquisite brick-built dome and simple mosaic cross when a concert is being performed there.

BEYAZIT AND FATİH

Chora Church
Kariye Müzesi, Kariye Camii Sokak, Edinekapı; tel: 0212-631 9241; Thur–Tue 9am–4.30pm; charge; bus: 31E from Eminönü; map p.114 B3
One of the truly great sights of İstanbul is the Chora Church even if not many visitors make it here. It originally stood in the fields just inside the city walls. Today it's surrounded by housing, some of it pretty and wooden, and looks like a small local Byzantine church. It's only once you cross the threshold that you appreciate its magnificence because this was a church that was completely redecorated with

Below: the tower of St Stephen of the Bulgars.

Since the attacks on Neve Shalom in 1986, 1992 and 2003 it has been very difficult to see inside İstanbul's surviving synagogues. If you wish to do so you must apply in writing to the Chief Rabbi in Büyük Hendek Sokak, Galata (tel: 0212-244 1980) and fax through a copy of your passport details.

İskele Mosque
İskele Camii, Demokrasi Meydanı, Üsküdar; ferry: Üsküdar
This is an unmissable large mosque that originally stood right on the waterfront but is now across the road from the ferry terminal. It was designed by Sinan in 1547 for one of the daughters of Sultan Süleyman the Magnificent.

Şakirin Mosque
Şakirin Camii, Şehit Ahmet Deresi Yolu, Karacaahmet; ferry: Harem, then 20-minute walk
Proof that it is still possible to build an interesting new mosque, the Şakirin, built in 2009 with its amazing arched mihrab of turquoise and gold, a mimber decorated with stylized leaves, and a chandelier of dripping plastic adorned, will come as a relief to those

who crave a little originality in their mosques. The interior design was created by a woman best known for her work on some of the city's most upmarket restaurants.

SYNAGOGUES

EMİNÖNÜ AND THE GOLDEN HORN

Ahrida Synagogue
Vodina Caddesi 9, Balat; ferry: Balat, then 15-minute walk; map p. 114 C3
The finest of the city's surviving synagogues dating back to 1694 with a wonderful internal dome of wood and a magnificent *bema* (prayer platform) that some believe is intended to evoke Noah's Ark.

CHURCHES

SULTANAHMET AND KUMKAPI

Church of St Eirene
Aya İrini, Topkapı Palace; only open for concerts; tram: Sultanahmet; map p.121 D2
It may be Aya Sofya (Holy Wisdom) that grabs the headlines but smaller Aya İrini (Holy Peace), in the grounds of the Topkapı Palace, is exactly the same age; both are

Right: the Greek Patriarchate
is the mother church of the
Greek Orthodoxy.

Most of İstanbul's churches
are kept locked behind high
walls guarded by security
cameras. Your best chance to
see inside most of them is on
a Sunday morning.

glittering mosaics and
dramatic frescoes in the
late 13th century when the
Byzantine emperor had
recovered Constantinople
from the Crusaders who
held it from 1204 to 1261.
The narthex is filled with
mosaic images of the life
of Christ and his mother
Mary, while the pareccle-
sion chapel boasts fres-
coes of the Last
Judgement and the Har-
rowing of Hell. The man
responsible for all this
splendour was Theodore
Metochites who appears
in one of the mosaics in a
hat that wouldn't look out
of place at Ascot.

EMİNÖNÜ AND THE
GOLDEN HORN

Greek Patriarchate

Patrikhane, Sadrazam Ali Paşa
Caddesi, Fener; tel: 0212-531
9670; www.ec-patr.org; daily
9am–5pm; ferry: Fener; map
p.115 D2

Still the mother church of
Greek Orthodoxy, the
Patriarchate has a history
stretching right back to
Byzantium although the
current church on the site
only dates from 1720. It's
dimly-lit interior gives a
great feeling of what it
might have been like to
attend a service in the
Middle Ages. Several
obscure saints are
interred in caskets in the
south aisle.

St Stephen
of the Bulgars

Sveti Stefan Kilisesi, Mürsel
Paşa Caddesi, Fener; tel: 0212-
521 1121; Mon–Sat 9am–5pm;
free; ferry: Fener; map p.115
C3

A rare example of a church
completely created out of
cast iron, St Stephen's is a
surreal piece of Gothic
Revival architecture built in
Vienna in 1871 and then
shipped down the Danube
in pieces to be recreated
on the banks of the
Golden Horn.

BEYOĞLU

Aya Triada

İstiklal Caddesi, Meşelik
Sokağı; funicular: Taksim; map
p.117 C3

Looming over Burger Kong
and the kebab stands of
İstiklal Caddesi is the enormous church of the Holy
Trinity, designed by the
Greek architect Vasilaki
Ioannidi in 1880 and the
first church in the city to
sport a dome after laws
forbidding such ostenta-
tion on Christian buildings
were lifted. Usually only
the narthex is open but on
a Sunday you may be able
to see the capacious, light-
filled interior.

St Anthony's Cathedral

İstiklal Caddesi; www.sentan
tuan.com; Mon–Sat 8am–6pm
and Sun services; free; funicular: Tünel, then 10-minute walk;
map p.116 B3

Set back from busy İstiklal
Caddesi, this unexpected
piece of Italian Gothic
Revival was designed by
Giulio Mongeri in 1906. A
Catholic church, it is by
far the busiest and most
active of the city's non-
Orthodox churches.

Crimean Memorial
Church (Christ Church)

Krim Kilisesi, Serdar-ı Ekrem
Caddesi, Tünel; tel: 0212-251
5616; Mon–Sat 9am–5pm;
charge; funicular: Tünel; map.
p.116 B2

Designed by G.E. Street
of London Law Courts
fame, this church was
built to commemorate the
dead of the Crimean War
in 1858 and restored in
the 1990s. It is a little
piece of England trans-
ferred to İstanbul and
contains a colourful
rood screen by the
Scottish artist Mungo
McCosh that includes
scenes and personalities
familiar to 21st-century
İstanbul expats.

83

Mosques, Synagogues & Churches

Museums and Galleries

As befits a city with so much history İstanbul has more than its fair share of museums, some of them very well known and visited, others virtually ignored. The two big must-sees are the İstanbul Archeology Museum and the Museum of Turkish and Islamic Arts. Aya Sofya, too, is technically a museum but most visitors probably see it as a church-turned-mosque. It was only relatively recently that the city acquired a world-class art gallery in the İstanbul Modern, but now the city's arts scene is booming.

SULTANAHMET AND KUMKAPI

Great Palace Mosaics Museum

Mozaik Müzesi, Torun Sokak, Sultanahmet; tel: 0212-518 1205; Tue–Sun 9.30am–4.30pm; charge; tram: Sultanahmet; map p.121 D1
Preserved in situ, this magnificent stretch of mosaic pavement from the Great Palace depicts a variety of scenes from everyday life in Byzantium, including a man milking a goat, children herding ducks and a bear up a tree. It's made up of an estimated 75–80 million tesserae and probably dates back to the sixth century and the reign of Justinian the Great.

İstanbul Archeology Museum

Osman Hamdi Bey Yokuşu, Gülhane Park; tel: 0212-520 7740; Tue–Sun 9am–5pm; charge: tram: Gülhane; map p.121 D2
A museum in three separate parts within the same complex, this is a wonderful place that deserves at

Above: in the İstanbul Archeology Museum.

least half a day of your time. The most interesting part is actually called the Archaeology Museum and is housed inside a fine porticoed building. You should head immediately for the rooms containing a series of sarcophagi brought here from the Sidon necropolis (now in Lebanon); the most impressive is called the Alexander Sarcophagus because of the lovely carvings of the great leader on its sides, but the others are

almost equally magnificent. Also in this part of the museum are Classical sculptures collected from archaeological sites around the country. Upstairs you'll find artefacts from all over what was the Ottoman Empire, while downstairs you shouldn't miss the cramped gallery that houses finds made during excavations for the Marmaray project, including stunning photographs of the medieval port at Yenikapı.

Left: the imposing structure of the Archeology Museum.

.30pm; charge; tram: Gülhane; map p.121 D3

This small, new museum illustrates the exceptionally important role played by the Middle East in scientific history. Most of the exhibits are replicas, but they are beautifully displayed, and amongst other things you can find out about the long history of the İstanbul Observatory which now has responsibility for keeping track of earthquakes in an earthquake-prone city.

İstanbul's interesting smaller museums include a **Jewish Museum** (Perçemli Sokak, Karaköy; tel: 0212-292 6333; www.muze500.com; Mon–Thur 10am–4pm, Fri and Sun 10am–2pm; charge; tram: Karaköy; map p.116 B1), a **Toy Museum** (Göztepe Oyuncak Müzesi, Ömerpaşa Caddesi, Dr. Zeki Zeren Sokak, Göztepe; tel: 0216-359 4550; www.İstanbul oyuncakmuzesi.com; Tue–Sun 10am–5pm; charge) and a **Postal Museum** (Büyük Postane, Şehinşah Pehlevi Caddesi, Sirkeci; Mon–Fri 8am–5pm; free; tram: Sirkeci; map p.121 C3).

ion from which Sultan Mehmed the Conqueror could watch games of *cirit* (a form of polo), the Çinili Köşk is so called because of its lovely turquoise-tiled façade. Not surprisingly it is now used to house the museum's ceramics collection, including some exquisite examples of İznik ware from around the city.

Museum of the History of Islamic Science and Technology

Gülhane Park; tel: 0212-528 8065; Wed–Mon 9am–4-

Turkish and Islamic Arts Museum

At Meydanı, Sultanahmet: tel: 0212-512 0480; Wed–Mon 9am–5pm; charge; tram: Sultanahmet; map p.121 C1

Housed inside what was once the palace of İbrahim Paşa, the favourite of Sultan Süleyman the Magnificent, this museum, of which the wonderful building is almost one of the exhibits, is famous for its stunning collection of carpets, including a series of pieces from Uşak that now hang from ceiling to floor. Aside from the carpets there is also some wonder-

Below: fascinating exhibits at the Mosaics Museum.

The second building houses the Museum of the Ancient Orient whose most treasured possession is the Kadesh Treaty, a cuneiform record of a peace agreement between the Egyptians and the Hittites dating back to the 13th century BC. The third building, the Çinili Köşk (Tiled Pavilion), is the most beautiful to look at. Originally built as a pavil-

ful ceramic and glassware, as well as a magnificent medieval door removed from a mosque in Cizre in the southeast. In the basement the ethnography section includes many artefacts from Turkey's now largely lost nomadic way of life, as well as dioramas showing life around the country at different dates.

BEYAZIT AND FATİH
Fethiye Museum
Fethiye Müzesi; Fethiye Kapısı Sokak, Fatih; Thur–Tue 9am–5pm; charge; bus: 38E from Eminönu, then 15-minute walk; map p.114 C2
The side chapel of what was originally the 13th-century Church of the Theotokos Pammakaristos built by Emperor John Comnenus and his wife Anna Doukaina is a little-visited gem, its walls and dome covered with the same sort of glittering mosaics that draw coach-loads of visitors to the better-known Chora Church. The rest of the church continues to serve as a mosque as it has done since the Ottoman conquest.

EMİNÖNÜ AND THE GOLDEN HORN
Rahmi M Koç Museum
Hasköy Caddesi 5, Hasköy; tel: 0212-369 6600; www.rmk-museum.org.tr; Tue–Fri 10am–5pm, Sat–Sun 10am–7pm; charge; ferry: Hasköy or bus 36T from Taksim; map p.115 C4
A museum likely to hold a great deal of appeal for children with a huge range of trains and boats and planes on display in an abandoned shipyard.
SEE ALSO CHILDREN, P.40

Santralistanbul
Kazım Karabekir Caddesi 2/6, Sütlüce; tel: 0212-311 7809; www.santralistanbul.com; Tue–Sun 10am–8pm; charge; ferry: Sütlüce, then 20-minute walk
For those who like their art cutting edge Santralistanbul is housed inside a decommissioned power station and hosts changing exhibitions of whatever is currently hot.

KARAKÖY, TOPHANE AND BEŞİKTAŞ
İstanbul Modern
Meclis-i Mebusan Caddesi, Tophane; tel: 0212-334 7300; www.istanbulmodern.org; Tue–Wed, Fri–Sun 10am-6pm, Thur

10am–8pm; charge (free Thur); tram: Tophane; map p.116 C2
The wonderful light-filled İstanbul Modern occupies an old warehouse on the waterfront at Tophane which guarantees amazing Bosphorus views to supplement the art. Turkish art in the Western sense of paintings only really dates back to the 19th century and the gallery has a fine and representative collection that is put on display in rotation. Names to look out for include Burhan Doğançay, Nuri İrem, Fahrelnissa Zeid, Osman Hamdi Bey and Hamit Görele. The basement plays host to temporary exhibitions of art and photography.

Naval Museum
Beşiktaş Meydanı, Beşiktaş; tel: 0212-327 4345; www.dzkk.tsk.tr; Wed–Sun 9am–5pm; charge; bus: 25RE from Kabataş; map p.117 E4
Undergoing major refurbishment at the time of writing, the Naval Museum is home to magnificent examples of the graceful caiques, gondola-like boats in which the sultan and his entourage would be rowed around the Bosphorus.

BEYOĞLU
Pera Museum
Pera Müzesi, Meşrutiyet Caddesi 65, Tepebaşı; tel: 0212-334 9900; www.peramusezi.org.tr; Tue–Sat 10am–7pm, Sun noon–6pm; charge; funicular: Tünel; map p.116 B3
State-of-the-art museum with permanent collections of Kütahya ceramics and medieval weights that are

Left: in the exciting İstanbul Modern museum.

of rather specialist interest but which also houses many early landscape images of the city as well as Osman Hamdi Bey's much-copied masterpiece 'The Tortoise Trainer'. The upper floors are often used for blockbuster visiting exhibitions.

NİŞANTAŞI, TEŞVİKİYE AND MAÇKA
Military Museum
Askeri Müzesi, Valikonağı Caddesi, Harbiye; tel: 0212-233 2720; Wed–Sun 9am–5pm; charge; Metro: Osmanbey
The finest exhibits in the Military Museum are the elaborate tents which provided temporary homes for sultans on manoeuvres, but you can also see a piece of the chain that used to be strung across the Golden Horn to prevent ships entering it.
SEE ALSO CHILDREN, P.41

THE BOSPHORUS
Sadberk Hanım Museum
Piyasa Caddesi 25-9, Büyükdere; tel: 0212-242 3813; www. sadberkhanimmuzesi.org.tr; Thur–Tue 10am–5pm; charge; bus: 25RE from Kabataş
Way up the Bosphorus and so attracting relatively few visitors, this fine private museum contains a beautifully displayed archaeological collection as well as a magnificent ethnography section with dioramas to show the rituals associated with engagement, marriage and circumcision. Most of the embroideries on display are exquisite. It is housed inside a restored *yalı* (wooden waterside mansion).

Sakıp Sabancı Museum
Sakıp Sabancı 22, Emirgan; tel: 0212-277 2200; www.muze. sabanciuniv.edu; Wed–Sat 10am–6pm; charge; bus: 25RE from Kabataş
Beautifully located in a fine mansion in a hillside garden overlooking the Bosphorus, the Sakıp Sabancı was once a private home and some of the rooms are set up to show off antique furniture and paintings. Others house a fine collection of calligraphy. The Sabancı has established itself as *the* venue for big touring exhibitions by the likes of Picasso and Dali. Check *Time Out İstanbul in English* for details.

GREATER İSTANBUL
Panorama 1453
Topkapı Park, Topkapı; tel: 0212-467 0700; daily 8.30am–7pm; charge; tram: Pazartekke
This new museum contains a 360-degree representation of the struggle between the Ottomans and Byzantines for Constantinople in 1453 complete with sound and light effects. It should help you inject some life into the dry bones of the history of the nearby city walls. Please note that this Topkapı is nowhere near Topkapı Palace.

Yedikule
Kule Meydanı, Samatya; tel: 0212-584 4012; daily 9am–6.30pm; charge; train; Yedikule
Just inland from the Sea of Marmara, Yedikule is a collection of seven towers (which is what its name means in Turkish) that played much the same role in Ottoman history as the Tower of London did in British history as a prison and the place where less fortunate rulers (in this case Young Osman) came to violent ends. Sadly, nothing has been done to capitalise on its history so you can only wander in and out of the towers and do your best to imagine their grisly past.

> Most İstanbul museums close on Mondays, making Friday to Sunday a better bet for a long sightseeing weekend than Saturday to Monday. In higher summer some stay open until early evening, but most state-owned museums chase visitors out very promptly by 5pm.

Music, Film and Dance

Istanbul has a thriving cultural life, encompassing all the main art forms. For non-Turkish-speakers theatre is something of a closed book but everyone will find something to suit their musical tastes, be it classical or pop, Turkish or international. Turkish cinema has a history dating back to the 1950s and after a period in the relative doldrums film makers are starting to make a splash internationally, picking up regular awards at international festivals.

CLASSICAL MUSIC

SULTANAHMET AND KUMPKAPI

Aya İrini

Topkapı Palace, Sultanahmet; tram: Sultanahmet; map p.121 D2

Only used during İstanbul's music festivals *(see p.48)*, Aya İrini, one of the oldest Byzantine churches in the city, is also one of the city's most romantic and atmospheric venues for a wide variety of music.

NİŞANTAŞI, TEŞVİKİYE AND MAÇKA

Cemal Reşit Rey Concert Hall (CRR)

Gümüş Sokak, Harbiye; tel: 0212-232 9830; www.crrks.org; box office 10am-7.30pm; funicular: Taksim, then 20-min walk

CRR may be a more conventional concert venue but it is also comfortable and has great acoustics.

Lütfü Kırdar Concert Hall

Darülbedai Sokak, Harbiye; tel: 0212-296 3055; www.ice.org; funicular: Taksim, then 20-min walk

Above: a concert at Aya İrini.

Home to the Borusan İstanbul Philharmonic Orchestra, this hall is also used during the Efes Pilsen Blues Festival in autumn.

JAZZ

BEYOĞLU

Jazz Club

Hasnun Galip Sokak 14; tel: 0212-245 0516; www.jazzcafeİstanbul.com; Tue–Fri 8pm–4am (closed July & August); funicular: Taksim, then 10-min walk; map p.116 C3

This is a long-lived jazz venue which also plays host to other types of music on Tuesdays and Thursdays.

Nardis Jazz Club

Kulesi Sokak 14, Galata; tel: 0212-244 6327; www.nardis-jazz.com; Mon–Thu 8pm–1am, Fri–Sat 8pm–2am; funicular: Tünel; map p.116 B1

Cosy and very popular club in the shadow of the Galata Tower which offers twice-nightly peformances as well as decent food. Run by a jazz guitarist and his wife.

POP

NİŞANTAŞI, TEŞVİKİYE AND MAÇKA

Cemil Topuzlu Harbiye Open Air Theatre

Taşkışla Caddesi, Harbiye; tel: 0212-232 8603; funicular: Taksim, then 20-min walk; map p.116 B1

This is a large amphitheatre that can accommodate up to 4,500 people and generally caters for big-name pop concerts.

THE BOSPHORUS

Türkcell Kuruçeşme Arena

Muallim Naci 60, Kuruçeşme; tel: 0212-263 3983; www.turkcellkurucesmearena.com; bus:

Left: catch a performance by Whirling Dervishes

For the most authentic Whirling Dervish performances, visit the Galata Dervish Lodge (Galata Mevlevihane, Galipdede Caddesi 15, Tünel; tel: 212-245 4141; Wed–Mon 9.30am–5pm, check board outside for performance times; charge; map p.116 B2).

KADIKÖY AND ÜSKÜDAR

Rexx
Sakızgülü Sokak 20-22, Kadıköy; tel: 0212-336 0112; www.rexx-online.com; ferry: Kadıköy, then 20-minute walk

DANCE
Dance of Colours
Firat Cultural Centre, Divan Yolu, Çemberlitaş; tel: 0554-797 2646; www.dancesofcolour.com; Thur 7.30pm; tram: Çemberlitaş; map p.120 C2
Even if the idea of the sort of Turkish night where belly-dancing is the main dish on the menu doesn't appeal to you you might like to drop in on this venue, within walking distance of Sultanahmet, to watch a performance of folkloric dancing from all around the country. You won't forget the 'sardine dance' from Trabzon on the Black Sea in a hurry.

Below: the Nardis Jazz Club is deservedly popular.

Türkü is a popular style of music that gives a contemporary flavour to traditional songs. Lively bars offering türkü music can be found on either side of the Taksim end of İstiklal Caddesi. Expect the audiences to be word perfect and enthusiastic.

25RE from Kabataş
Waterside venue for concerts by the likes of Teoman and Ajda Pekkan, as well as international acts like Sting and Shakira.

FILM
Turkish cinema has been on a roll recently with directors such as Nuri Bilge Ceylan finding international success with films such as Üç Maymun ('Three Monkeys'). Other names to conjure with include Ferzan Özpetek whose 1997 film Hamam ('Steam') was a critical and commercial success; and Çagan Irmak whose 2008 film Issız Adam ('Alone') was almost as popular for its soundtrack as for its script. Although Turkey does produce some action movies such as 2004's Kurtlar Vadisi Iraq, a spin-off from a popular TV series, and comedies such as 2006's Dondurmam Gaymak ('Ice Cream I Scream'), most of its output is heavy on drama and sentiment with a liberal helping of politics, a tradition largely established by the much revered Yılmaz Güney whose Yol ('The Way') won the Palme d'Or at the Cannes Film Festival in 1982.

SULTANAHMET AND KUMKAPI

Şafak Sinemaları
Divan Yolu 134, Çemberlitaş; tel: 0212-516 2660; tram: Çemberlitaş; map p.121 C2

BEYOĞLU
AFM Fitaş
İstiklal Caddesi 24–6; tel: 0212-444 1136; www.afm.com.tr; funicular: Taksim; map p.116 C3

Atlas Sinemaları
İstiklal Caddesi 209; tel: 0212-252 8576; funicular: Taksim; map p.116 B2

Nightlife

Forget any worries about İstanbul being in a Muslim country. The city has a thriving nightlife which sees the action going on well into the small hours. It's at its liveliest in winter since many of the best clubs relocate to coastal resorts in summer. The exceptions are the small clubs and bars around Taksim and the big club-restaurant complexes along the Bosphorus where the cooling sight of the water is enough to make up for the heat. Alcohol is expensive, though, so expect to pay dearly for your pleasure. Certainly at the Bosphorus venues you should also dress the part if you want to get past the doormen.

SULTANAHMET AND KUMKAPI

Red River Pub

Hüdavendigar Caddesi 44, Gülhane; tel: 0212-513 7310; www.redriverpub.com; daily 10am–midnight; tram: Gülhane; map p.121 D3

It looks like an English pub, it serves the same sort of food but it's actually an American West-themed bar just with wide-screen screen television thrown in so you can watch all your favourite teams from back home.

Sultan Pub

Divan Yolu 2, Sultanahmet; tel: 0212-528 1719; daily 9.30am–1pm; tram: Sultanahmet; map p.121 D2

Street-corner café-restaurant that fancies itself as an English pub and serves a decent repertoire of pub staples and ice-cold beer to weary sightseers.

BEYOĞLU

Babylon

Seyhbender Sokak 3, Tünel; tel: 0212-292 7368; www.babylon. com; Tue–Thur 9.30pm–2am, Fri–Sat 10pm–3am (closed July & August); funicular: Tünel; map p.116 B2

Best of all the live music venues in İstanbul, Babylon boasts world-class acoustics and DJs and plays host to a wonderfully exotic mix of acts from the likes of punk queen Patti Smith through to Mercan Dede who has given a techno twist to traditional Sufi music particularly focused on the *ney* (flute).

Ghetto

Kalyoncu Kulluk Caddesi 10, Galatasaray; tel: 0212-251 7501; www.ghettoist.com; daily 8am–4pm (closed July & August); funicular: Tünel; map p.116 B3

In a former bakery, this high-ceilinged, dingy-black venue hosts a range of

When it comes to imaginative nightlife options Sultanahmet is not really where it's at. That said, Akbıyık Caddesi, a street lined with hostels and hotels, is packed with pavement bars where the booze is cheap and closing time late.

Below: Babylon is the place to go for live music.

Left: young İstanbul heads out on the town.

For a taste of boho, student İstanbul nightlife hop straight on a ferry to Kadıköy and head off in search of Kadife Sokak (AKA Barlar Caddesi – Bar Street) where a series of pretty wooden houses have been turned into themed bars. Karga (Crow) has been in business a long time but Masal Evi (Fairytale House) has the edge if you're after colourful and pretty décor.

local and international acts. Its roof terrace becomes the Peymane restaurant in summer when Ghetto itself skips town.

Indigo
Mısr Apartments, İstiklal Caddesi, Galatasaray; tel: 0212-245 1307; www.livingindigo.com; funicular: Tünel; map p.116 B2
The place to come if you're into cutting-edge electronic and dance music with a Turkish twist. Several floors of boisterous action.

Jolly Joker Balans
İstiklal Caddesi, Balo Sokak 22; tel: 0212-251 7762; www.jolly

Below: the Suada club is a glamorous hotspot.

jokerbalans.com; 10pm–3pm (closed August); funicular: Taksim; map p.116 B3
With something of the feel of an outsize Irish pub, the Jolly Joker provides entertainment with a wide range of local artistes and serves, in its caramel brew, what is said to be one of the finest beers in town.

Roxy
Aslan Yatağı Sokak 5; tel: 0212-249 1283; www.roxy.com.tr; Fri–Sat 10pm–4am (closed July & August); funicular: Tünel; map p.116 C3
Grungier version of Babylon that also hosts the YAN Gastrobar.

THE BOSPHORUS
Reina
Muallim Naci Caddesi 10, Ortaköy; tel: 0212-259 5919; www.reina.com.tr; daily 6pm–4am; bus: 25RE from Kabataş
Its 2009 guest list recorded visits from the likes of Sting, Paris Hilton and Kevin Costner which rather suggests how exclusive a venue this is. Charge up your credit card and bear

in mind that if you can't afford to sweep in from the waterside you might not feel at your most comfortable here.

Sortie
Muallim Nacı Caddesi 141, Ortaköy; tel: 0212-327 8585; www.sortie.com.tr; daily 6pm–4am; bus: 25RE from Kabataş
İstanbul's 'see-and-be-seen' venue par excellence where you really will need the glad rags to get through the front door (those with the real money arrive by boat of course). Sortie is as much a place to eat as a club; the dancing only gets going after midnight.

Suada
Kuruçeşme; tel: 0212-263 7300; www.suadaclub.com.tr; daily 6pm–4am; bus: 25RE from Kabataş, then ferry from Kuruçeşme Park
It bills itself as 'the island between two continents' and what could be more romantic than dancing the night away at this upmarket club with a choice of six excellent restaurants on what is really an islet belonging to the Galatasaray football club?

91

Palaces

The most important palace in İstanbul is Topkapı, the treasure-chest that was home to the sultans for around 400 years. It's the best place in the city to get a feel for the days under leaders such as Süleyman I as well as to imagine the scandal and mayhem of the Harem. In the mid-19th century Topkapı was abandoned in favour of the more modern Dolmabahçe Palace on the other side of the Golden Horn, only to be abandoned as Sultan Abdülhamid took refuge inland in the Yıldız Palace. Smaller palaces such as Beylerbeyi, Küçüksu and Ihlamur were used as summer homes or to rest on long journeys.

SULTANAHMET AND KUMKAPI

Topkapı Palace

Topkapı Sarayı, Babıhümayun Caddesi; tel: 0212-512 0480; www.topkapisarayi.gov.tr; Wed–Mon 9am–5pm; charge (separate charge for Harem); tram: Sultanahmet; map p.121 E3

The extraordinary Topkapı Palace is nothing like the idea of a palace lodged in the minds of people who've visited places like Buckingham Palace in London. Instead it is more like the Alhambra in Spain, a wonderful gathering of pretty courtyards surrounded with porticoes and dotted with pavilions that look out on the glittering expanse of the Sea of Marmara at the point where it merges with the Bosphorus and the Golden Horn. Here it was that the sultans not only lived but also presided over the business of state, keeping an eye on what went on in the *Divan* (Council Chamber) through a peephole high in the wall.

The palace grounds are divided into four courtyards each with particular points of interest. The first courtyard is more like an enclosed park that anyone can wander into. Its most conspicuous monument is the church of Aya İrini, virtually contemporary with Aya Sofya but only open to visitors as a concert hall. It's in the first courtyard that you buy a ticket to pass through the Gate of Salutations to the second courtyard and the parts of the palace that would only ever have been accessible to those with specific reason to be there. The second courtyard is ringed with porticoes like the cloister of a medieval cathedral. One area displays a collection of imperial carriages, while a gateway leads through to the many-chimneyed kitchens that are now used to house collections of porcelain and siverware. To the left of the courtyard is the double-chambered *Divan* where grand viziers

would once have administered justice. Accessible through a surprisingly inconspicuous doorway beside it is the Harem.

Despite all the fevered speculation engendered by thoughts of the sultan's multiple concubines, the Harem was really just the private quarters of the palace, a place run along strict hierarchical lines and guarded by eunuchs who held great power. Inside you'll find a succession of

Left: Topkapı Palace is one of the city's major attractions.

alds the size of eggs, golden thrones studded with rubies, and of course the famous Topkapı Dagger that played a leading role in the movie 'Topkapı' – they're all here along with the predictable crowds waiting to view them.

Finally you arrive in the fourth courtyard which doesn't really feel like a courtyard at all because much of it opens onto spectacular watery views. Here, though, you'll find some of the prettiest pavilions built by the sultans to commemorate military victories in what are now Iraq and Armenia, as well as a beautifully tiled chamber where the young sultans were circumcised and a delightful platform where their fathers would have broken their fast during Ramadan while gazing out over one of the finest views of the city.

Topkapı is too good to rush. Make sure you allow at least half a day and preferably more to do it justice. There's a restaurant and café in the fourth courtyard.

KARAKÖY, TOPHANE AND BEŞİKTAŞ

Dolmabahçe Palace

Dolmabahçe Sarayı, Dolmabahçe Caddesi, Beşiktaş; tel: 0212-236 9000; www.dolmabahce.gov.tr; Tue–Wed, Fri–Sun 9am–4pm; charge (guided tours only); tram: Kabataş; map p.117 E4
Dolmabahçe conforms more closely to what most visitors will expect of a palace in that it is primarily one large structure, albeit with two separate

On the banks of the Golden Horn at Kasımpaşa stands one other imperial palace, the Aynalıkavak Kasrı. It contains a wonderful ceiling dating back to the 18th century but has been closed for restoration for many years.

unexpectedly small living rooms as well as a huge Imperial Hall that would have been used on ceremonial occasions. Treats to look out for include the

glorious marble and gold *hamam* suite and the delightful Fruit Room of Sultan Ahmed III which is wallpapered with murals of fruit and flowers – it's just off the almost equally beautiful Salon of Murad III designed by the great Ottoman architect Sinan.

The exit from the Harem brings you out into the third courtyard which most visitors would have entered via the Gate of Felicity, bringing them face to face with the Throne Room where the sultan waited to receive gifts and greetings. This is one of the busiest parts of the palace complex since it's home to the imperial treasury and to the Sacred Safekeeping Hall which contains relics of the Prophet Mohammed. Even the most travel weary will find it hard not to be astounded by the wealth and magnificence on display in the treasury. Emer-

Left: the Topkapı Palace is ornately decorated.

93

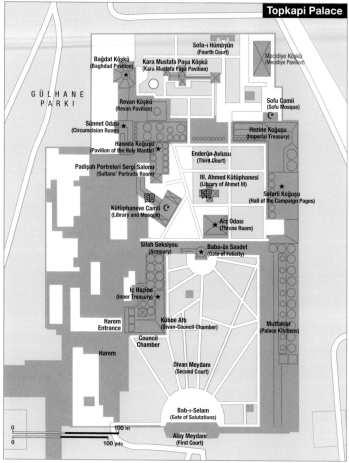

Topkapi Palace

Sofa-ı Hümâyûn (Fourth Court)

Bağdat Köşkü (Baghdad Pavilion) ★

Kara Mustafa Paşa Köşkü (Kara Mustafa Paşa Pavilion)

Mecidiye Köşkü (Mecidiye Pavilion)

G Ü L H A N E   P A R K I

Revan Köşkü (Revan Pavilion)

Sofu Camii (Sofu Mosque)

Sünnet Odası ★ (Circumcision Room)

Hazine Koğuşu (Imperial Treasury)

Hasoda Koğuşu (Pavilion of the Holy Mantle) ★

Padişah Portreleri Sergi Salonu (Sultans' Portraits Room)

Enderûn Avlusu (Third Court)

III. Ahmed Kütüphanesi (Library of Ahmet III)

Seferli Koğuşu (Hall of the Campaign Pages)

Kütüphaneve Camii (Library and Mosque)

Arz Odası ★ (Throne Room)

Silah Seksiyou (Armoury)

Baba-üs Saadet ★ (Gate of Felicity)

İç Hazine (Inner Treasury) ★

Harem Entrance

Kübbe Altı (Divan-Council Chamber)

Mutfaklar (Palace Kitchens)

Council Chamber

Harem

Divan Meydanı (Second Court)

Bab-ı-Selam (Gate of Salutations)

Alay Meydanı (First Court)

0 — 100 m
0 — 100 yds

---

entries, one for the Selamlık or men's part of the building, the other for the Haremlik or women's part. Sitting on reclaimed land right beside the Bosphorus, the Dolmabahçe is the handiwork of Garabet and Nikoğos Balyan, members of a prolific family of Ottoman Armenian architects. It took them from 1843 to 1856 to complete the work and when it was done the palace contained a mind-blowing 285 rooms and 43 halls but only six bathrooms.

The palace was designed in a Turkish version of Baroque. Unfortunately it was then stuffed to the gunnels with Bohemian crystal, Sevres porcelain, and gifts from other visiting monarchs so that some visitors will feel somewhat overwhelmed, especially as the compulsory guided tours leave little time to appreciate anything. No one, however, could fail to be impressed by the enormous Ceremonial Hall with its concealed dome – the room was so large that it took three days just to heat it. Equally impressive if on a much smaller scale is the room in which Atatürk, the first president of the country, died on 10 November 1938. His bed is draped with a Turkish flag and all the clocks in the palace are stopped at the moment of his death.

Above: rich Baroque-style furnishings at Dolmabahçe Palace.

Ihlamur Kasrı

Ortabahçe Caddesi, Beşiktaş; Tue–Wed, Fri–Sun 9am–4pm; charge (guided tours only); bus: 25RE from Kabataş, then 15-minute walk

Rarely visited by tourists, Ihlamur consists of a pair of pavilions, one for the men, the other for the women, set in a pretty small park with a lake. It's worth visiting to get a taste for Turkish Baroque without the overwhelming size or ever present crowds of Dolmabahçe.

THE BOSPHORUS

Beylerbeyi Palace

Beylerbeyi Sarayı, Abdullah Ağa Caddesi, Beylerbeyi; tel: 0216-321 9320; Tue–Wed, Fri–Sun 9am–5pm; charge (guided tours only); ferry: Beylerbeyi

Sitting in the shadow of the Bosphorus Bridge, Beylerbeyi Palace was built in Turkish Baroque style for Sultan Abdülaziz by Sarkis Balyan in 1865. It's like the Dolmabahçe

Palace in miniature but decorated with images of ships, a passion of the sultan, and with a wonderful indoor pool decorated with marble dolphins intended to offer an illusion of coolness to those stuck inside on hot days. The palace grounds are very beautiful and will be more so once work on restoring them is completed.

Küçüksu Kasrı

Küçüksu Caddesi, Kandilli; tel: 0216-332 3303; Tue–Wed, Fri–Sun 9am–4pm; charge (guided tours only); ferry: Anadolu Hisarı or Kandilli, then 15-minute walk

Of all İstanbul's 19th-century palaces perhaps the prettiest and most manageable is Küçüksu Kasrı whose eight rooms exemplify all the features of the Baroque style without becoming oppressive. The stairwell in particular is delightful. Don't miss the lovely Mihrişah Sultan Fountain in the grounds that dates back to 1807.

Right: Beylerbeyi Palace is perched on the water's edge.

95

Parks, Gardens and Beaches

For a very built-up city İstanbul actually has quite a lot of green spaces even though some are behind high walls so that visitors sometimes miss them. The best parks are relics of what were once estates reserved for the sultans but the biggest single green space is Belgrade Forest to the northwest of the city. İstanbul's beaches are not as good as those elsewhere in Turkey but for people staying in the city for a while it's worth knowing that you can escape to the sea at Kilyos. *See also Views and Walks, p.110.*

PARKS

SULTANAHMET AND KUMKAPI

Gülhane Park
Sultanahmet; tram: Gülhane; map p.121 D3
No visitor to Sultanahmet should leave without taking a turn round beautiful Gülhane Park which once formed part of the outer grounds of Topkapı Palace. A long lane of trees marches through the centre but if you wander off it you will find a rose garden, a Cypriot garden, a column dating back to Byzantine times and a series of wonderful tea gardens overlooking the Sea of Marmara.

Here, too, is the Museum of the History of Islamic Science and Technology. Herons nest in the park, green parakeets fly screeching across it. Come at tulip time to see it at its best. It might be best, however, to avoid the park on Sundays when half of İstanbul descends for a promenade.

Above: in Yıldız Park.

SEE ALSO MUSEUMS AND GALLERIES, P.85; PALACES, P.92; WALKS AND VIEWS, P.110

KARAKÖY, TOPHANE AND BEŞİKTAŞ

Yıldız Park
Beşiktaş; bus: 25RE from Kabataş
Concealed behind high walls, Yıldız Park was originally the grounds of Yıldız Palace, the last refuge of the paranoid Sultan Abdülhamid II. Trickling down a steep hillside, it is dotted with kiosks where you can stop off for a refreshing glass of tea – the Çadır Köşk (Tent Pavilion) overlooks a small lake while the Malta Köşk (Malta Pavilion) contains a wonderful indoor pool decorated with marble swans. It's a great place for a picnic though you need to be a little careful when scouting out a quiet corner since the park is very popular with lovers in search of somewhere to hide.

THE BOSPHORUS

Emirgan Woods
Emirgan; bus: 25RE from Kabataş
A short walk inland from the shore Emirgan Woods is another park on a slope with great views out over the Bosphorus. Of the historic pavilions inside it the finest is the Sarı Köşk (Yellow Pavilion), built to resemble a Swiss chalet and serving some decent food at very reasonable prices. Like Gülhane Park, Emirgan is at its beautiful best in tulip season when it can be very busy.

Left: tulips in full bloom in Emirgan Woods.

area is at Neşetsuyu near Bahçeköy, clearly signposted around the forest. The forest gets very busy with local families over summer weekends. It's at its most beautiful in autumn.

GARDENS

BEYAZIT AND FATİH

Botanical Garden
İstanbul University, Süleymaniye; Mon–Fri 9am–5pm; free; tram: Beyazıt, then 20-minute walk; map p.120 B4
İstanbul's small botanical garden is not especially well maintained and is of rather specialist interest. Casual visitors will probably be more impressed by the fantastic view of the confluence of the Sea of Marmara, the Bosphorus and the Golden Horn.

BEACHES
Solar Beach
Kilyos; tel: 0212-201 2612, www.solarbeach.org; charge; bus: 151 from Sarıyer
Fine stretch of sand that is used for concerts and summer festivities.

Seanergy
Gümüşdere, Kilyos; tel: 0212-203 0863; www.seanergytt.com; charge; bus: 151 from Sarıyer
This is a similarly inviting beach with a fish restaurant and a large stage for concerts.

The parks are very popular in April when the tulips are in bloom. However, they are almost equally beautiful in May when the lovely pink-blossomed Judas trees come into bloom.

The waters of the Black Sea at Kilyos have a treacherous undertow. It's wise only to swim in view of lifeguards.

GREATER İSTANBUL
Belgrade Forest
Bahçeköy; dolmuş: Büyükdere to Bahçeköy, then short walk
Best appreciated with a car, the Belgrade Forest is a vast area of mainly deciduous woodland to

the northwest of İstanbul which was once one of the main sources of water for the city. As a result you can perk up your picnicking by going in search of the remaining aqueducts and reservoirs, some of them dating back to Byzantine times, some of them works of the great Ottoman architect Sinan, some of them just very beautiful. The main picnic

Below: İstanbul is fortunate to be near some sandy stretches.

Restaurants

It sometimes seems as if every other person in Istanbul earns their living from serving food. Whether you want a quick *döner kebap* or the sort of multi-course feast once served to sultans you will find ample choice. What's more, good food doesn't always have to be expensive especially if you steer clear of tourist areas where so-so food often attracts inflated prices and the chi-chi areas where locals willingly pay through the nose for the address and surroundings. Some of the restaurants in the luxury hotels have excellent reputations although you'll get more atmosphere if you venture further afield.

SULTANAHMET AND KUMKAPI

Balıkçı Sabahattin
Seyit Hasan Köyü Sokak 1, Cankurtaran; tel: 0212-458 1824; www.balikcisabahattin. com; daily noon–midnight; €€€€; train: Cankurtaran; map p.120 D1
Excellent fish meals can be had at this pavement restaurant that migrates inside a wooden house in winter in a part of Cankurtaran that still feels rawly authentic. Everything tastes super-fresh although you might be surprised by the size of the bill given the surroundings.

Doydoy
Şifa Hamamı Sokak 13, Sultanahmet; tel: 0212-517 15 88; www.doydoy-restaurant.com;

daily 8am–10pm; €; tram: Sultanahmet, then 15-min walk; map p.121 C1
This is a long-time budget travellers' favourite which serves all the standard Turkish staples (lentil soup, a range of kebabs and baklava) at commendably low prices. The restaurant is spread over four floors, it boasts a terrace with stunning views of the Blue Mosque.

Karadeniz Aile Pide ve Kebap Salonu
Hacı Tahsinbey Sokak 1; tel: 0212-528 6290; daily 11am–11pm; €; tram: Sultanahmet; map p.121 C2
Pide is the Turkish take on pizza, and this little restaurant that has been in business since the days of the hippy trail offers a great introduction. *Kaşarlı* is a cheese pizza, *sucuklu* is with garlic sausage, while *karışık* comes with a bit of everything.

Khorasani
Ticarethane Sokak 39–41; tel: 0212-519 5959; www.khoras

Above: fresh Turkish pizza-style *pide* bread.

anirestaurant.com; 9am–11.30pm; €€€; tram: Sultahahmet; map p.121 D2
The spicy cuisine of southeastern Turkey around Gaziantep is especially revered amongst gourmets, and this restaurant does an excellent job of dishing it up from premises that are unusually stylish for this part of town. Watch the chef grilling your kebab on the *ocakbaşı* at the front – it'll certainly get your appetite going.

Kor Agop
Ördekli Bakkal Sokak 7; tel:

Left: İstanbul's dining scene is booming.

turned-luxury hotel. The menu is determinedly international with not a kebab in sight. Come here, also, for a wonderful Sunday brunch with eggs in every shape and size, sushi and sashimi, swordfish carpaccio, fresh honey and cream and much, much more. The desserts are particularly impressive.

Sultanahmet Fish House

Prof. K. İsmail Gürkan Caddesi 14; tel: 0212-527 4441; www. sultanahmetfishhouse.com; daily 11am–11pm; €€€; tram: Sultahahmet; map p.121 D2

It may lack the outdoor tables of Balıkçı Sabahattin but the Sultanahmet Fish House dishes up equally tasty fish dishes including *tuzda balık* (fish baked in salt) as well as a melt-in-the-mouth dessert called *ırmak helvası* (semolina helva), all in very attractive surroundings.

Tarihi Sultanahmet Köftecisi Selim Usta

Divan Yolu 4; tel: 0212-511 3960; www.sultanahmetkoftesi. com; daily 11am–11pm; €; tram: Sultahahmet; map p.121 D2

Turkey's kebabs are famous worldwide but the other staple of the Turkish restaurant, *köfte* (meatballs), has not travelled so well, despite the fact that it makes a cheap and cheerful alternative to a burger. This *köfteci* on Divan Yolu is so popular that at times there are queues to get in. Eat your meatballs with *piyaz* (white beans), salad and half a loaf of bread washed down with *ayran* (yoghurt drink) like the locals.

> Alcohol is very expensive in Turkey so the easiest way to cut back on your eating out bills is to forego wine and spirits especially.

0212-517 2334; 11am–midnight; €€€; train: Kumkapı; map p.120 B1

'Blind Agop' is one of longest established of the many fish restaurants that ring the main square in Kumkapı. People come here for a lively night out with lots of live music and alcohol to wash down the *mezes* and fish. Keep an eye on your bill (and your belongings) and you should have a great time.

Mozaik

Divan Yolu, İncili Çavuş Sokak 1; tel: 0212-512 4177; www. mozaikrestaurant.com; 9am–midnight; €€€; tram: Sultahahmet; map p.120 D2

With tables spilling out from a wooden house, Mozaik is very much a fixture of this narrow street and offers a menu that mixes Turkish kebabs with more international favourites, including salads and pastas. Portions are generous and service attentive, making this one of the best choices in the area.

Seasons

Four Seasons Hotel. Tevkifhane Sokak 1; tel: 0212-638 8200; www.fourseasons.com; 7am–11pm; €€€€; tram: Sultanahmet; map p.121 D2

Widely regarded as one of the city's best hotel restaurants, Seasons is enclosed in a glass-house in the courtyard of this prison-

Below: prowling for scraps at Asitane *(see p.100).*

Right: Pandeli offers expensive but tasty food.

BEYAZIT AND FATİH

Asitane

Kariye Oteli, Kariye Camii Sokak 18, Edirnekapı; tel: 0212-635 7997; www.asitane restaurant.com; €€€€; noon–midnight; bus: from Eminönü; map p.114 B3

Of the several restaurants in İstanbul that advertise Ottoman as opposed to normal Turkish cuisine Asitane is surely queen. Its menu includes dishes created to celebrate the circumcision of one of Sultan Süleyman the Magnificent's sons which means unusual treats such as *badem çorbası* (almond soup) harking back to the days when the palace cooks were expert at creating recipes to tickle a sultan's palate. In summer you eat in a garden behind the hotel.

Şehzade Mehmed Sofrası

Şehzade Mosque Courtyard, Şehzadebaşı Caddesi, Fatih; tel: 0212-526 2668; daily 9am–11pm; €€; tram: Laleli–Üniversite, then 10-min walk; map p.120 A3

Settings for restaurants don't get much more historically appealing than this with a restaurant lurking inside what was once a *medrese* (seminary) attached to the Şehzade Mosque. It's a great place to try a *fıstıklı kebap* (pistachio kebab) followed by a pastry doused in syrup.

Siirt Şeref

İtfaiye Caddesi 4; tel: 0212-635 8085; daily 10am–11pm; €€; Laleli-Üniversite, then 15-min walk; map p.120 A4

There's only one reason to come here and that is to eat *büryan kebab* (pit-baked kebab), an especially succulent kebab served on flat bread with *ayran* (yoghurt drink) and perhaps a helping of delectable *perde pilav* (rice stuffed with chicken, walnuts and pine nuts inside a pastry case).

Subası Lokantası

Kılıçlar Sokak 48, Grand Bazaar; tel: 0212-522 4762; Mon–Sat 11am–5pm; €; tram: Çemberlitaş; map p.120 C2

Those in the know slip out of the Grand Bazaar at lunchtime to head for this small and frantic eatery whose walls are plastered with newspaper eulogies to its *sulu yemekleri* (stews) and *zeytinyağlı* (prepared in olive oil) dishes. The best choices are gone long before 2pm.

Tarihi Kurufasulyeci Süleymaniyeli

Prof. Sıddık Sami Onar Caddesi

> There are many different types of restaurant in İstanbul (although the word *restoran* exists in Turkish it is rarely used in names) ranging from *lokantas* which are the basic standard eating-places to be found in every neighbourhood through *köftecis* specialising in meatballs to *balık evis* (fish houses) and *meyhanes* (taverns).

11, Süleymaniye; tel: 0212-513 6219; www.kurufasulyeci.com; €; tram: Beyazıt, then 10-min walk; map p.120 B3

Turks just love their *kuru fasulye* (baked beans) and one of the best places to try them is in this historic eatery within the Süleymaniye Mosque complex. They're not just tasty and filling, but blissfully cheap too.

EMİNÖNÜ AND THE GOLDEN HORN

Hamdi Et Lokantası

Tahmis Caddesi, Kalçın Sokak 17, Eminönü; tel: 0212-528 0390; www.hamdirestorant. com.tr; €€€; daily noon–11pm; tram: Eminönü; map p.120 C4

Easy to overlook in busy Eminönü is this hugely popular meat restaurant where grills top the menu. The upstairs dining room has views of the Golden Horn and a few tables outside to appreciate them better. Even with a reservation you'll be lucky to land one.

Kömür Lokantası

Müstantik Sokak 33, Küçükmustafapaşa; tel: 0212-631 0192; www.komurlokantasi.com; daily 9am–8pm; €; bus: 44B or 99 from Eminönü; map p.115 D2

If you're curious about the cabbage-based cuisine of the Black Sea then this small *lokanta* is the perfect place to try it. Cabbage not your thing? Well, anything

Right: at the sophisticated and trendy 360.

with *hamsi* (anchovies) will make a good alternative.

Pandeli
Spice Market; tel: 0212-522 5534; www.pandeli.com.tr; Mon–Sat 11am–3pm; €€€; tram: Eminönü; map p.120 C3
Pandeli comes in for mixed reviews. The food is certainly tasty and the setting – a turquoise-tiled dining room above one of the Spice Market gates – lovely. The drawbacks are twofold: price and attitude. Come mentally prepared and you can still have an enjoyable lunch.

Tarihi Haliç İşkembecisi
Abdülezelpaşa Caddesi 315, Cibali; tel: 0212-534 9414; www.haliciskembecisi.com; daily 24hrs; €€; bus: 44B or 99 from Eminönü; map p.115 D2
İşkembe çorbası (tripe soup) is a well-known Turkish remedy for a hangover, and this Golden Horn stalwart doles it out to diners round the clock. Of course it also boasts a normal menu of Turkish kebabs, salads and stews for those for whom the cure sounds worse than the headache.

KARAKÖY, TOPHANE AND BEŞİKTAŞ
İstanbul Modern Café
Meclis-i Mebusan Caddesi, Tophane; tel: 0212-292 2612; Tue–Sun 10am–6pm (Thur 8pm); €€€; tram: Tophane; map p.116 C2
You've seen the paintings, now sit down in the glorious, light-filled café in the same building to relish a wonderful selection of international dishes over a panoramic view of the Bosphorus.

Karaköy Lokantası
Kemankeş Caddesi 133, Karaköy; tel: 0212-292 4455; Mon–Sat noon–midnight; €€; tram: Karaköy, then 10-min walk; map p.116 C1
What was once the Estonian embassy is now a delightful turquoise-tiled restaurant that calls itself a *lokanta* and keeps alive the tradition of the *esnaf lokantaları* (workers' cafés) by featuring a menu that changes on a daily basis. The dishes on offer are all Turkish, and despite its rather glam appearance prices are very reasonable.

Left: try a local delicacy, tripe soup, at Tarihi Haliç İşkembecisi

BEYOĞLU
360
Mısır Apartımanı, İstiklal Caddesi 311/32; tel: 0212-244 8192; www.360istanbul.com; daily noon–3pm, 7.30pm–2am; €€€€; funicular: Tünel: map p.116 B2
Restaurants don't get much trendier than 360 which took its name – surprise, surprise! – from the almost 360-degree views available from its terrace. This is a place where it pays to dress to kill before you sit down to its much-raved-about choice of international dishes. That said, visitors not dressed in Gucci and with child in tow have been pleasantly surprised at how welcome they were made to feel.

Canım Ciğerim
Minare Sokak 1, Asmalımescit; tel: 0212-252 6060; daily 10am–midnight; €; funicular: Tünel: map p.116 B2
Small corner *lokanta* where you can get the full south-

Price per person for a single meze platter and/or soup, a main course, and one drink, in euros:
€= under €10
€€ = €10-18
€€€ = €18-25
€€€€ = over €25

101

For a really wild night out you could do worse than head for Nevizade Sokak, the narrow street behind the Çiçek Pasajı off İstiklal Caddesi which is completely lined with *meyhanes* (taverns) where İstanbul residents in their hundreds dine out every night on trays of *mezes*, plateloads of fish and liberal doses of *rakı*. Gypsy musicians serenade the crowds until the early hours. Grab a table where you can get one – you're unlikely to go far wrong.

eastern Turkey *ciğer* (liver) experience, sitting down on stools at simple tables and nibbling your way through the contents of a handful of skewers, one of them sneakily loaded with neat lamb fat. Greenery, beetroots and *ayran* (yoghurt drink) come with.

Konak

İstiklal Caddesi 259, Galatasaray; tel: 0212-244 4281; daily 7.30am–11.30pm; €; funicular: Taksim; map p.116 B2

Döner kebap is the bog-standard meat dish served from a vertical grill, *İskender kebap* its more upmarket cousin, the meat loaded onto a bed of soft *pide* bread and accompanied with a dollop of

yoghurt and a drizzle of tomato and butter sauces. It's the mouth-watering staple of Konak, which is sprouting branches all along İstiklal Caddesi.

Leb-i Derya

İstiklal Caddesi, Kumbaracı Yokuşu 115/7; tel: 0212-293 4989; www.lebiderya.com; Mon–Fri 11am–2am, Sat–Sun 8.30am–3am; €€€€; funicular: Tünel: map p.116 B2

It started as a delightful bar with stunning Bosphorus views and evolved into a restaurant with such a loyal fan base that it rapidly outgrew this original address. Come here or to its sister branch in the Richmond Hotel to dine on a carefully prepared choice of international favourites in stylish surroundings.

Lokal

İstiklal Caddesi, Müeyyet Sokak 9; tel: 0212-245 5743; noon–11pm; €€€; funicular: Tünel: map p.116 B2

The homely little Lokal (which is Turkish for canteen) wields its fusion menu of Thai, Chinese and Indonesian fishes with aplomb. With space at a premium you'd be wise to book ahead. The acoustics indoors don't exactly encourage conversation.

Mikla

The Marmara Pera, Meşrutiyet Caddesi 117, Tepebaşı; tel: 0212-293 5656; www.mikla restaurant.com; Mon–Sat 6.30pm–1am; €€€€; funicular: Tünel: map p.116 B2

On the top floor of The Marmara Pera hotel Mikla boasts one of the best views in town and a menu of beautifully prepared and presented dishes that mix and match Turkish and international flavours. Its *hamsi* (anchovy) crisps are a unique delight.

Yakup 2

Çukurlu Çeşme Sokak 13, Asmalımescit; tel: 0212-249 2925; daily noon–midnight; €€€; funicular: Tünel: map p.117 C3

When it comes to *meyhanes* (taverns) you don't get much more popular than Yakup 2 which attracts a devoted local following of chattering-class types for a *meze* table that includes delectable *ahtapot* (octopus) and *fava* (mashed broad beans). Oh, and the grills to follow are pretty hot too.

Zencefil

İstiklal Caddesi, Karabiye Sokak 8, Taksim; tel: 0212-243 8234; Mon–Sat 10am–10pm; €€€; funicular: Taksim; map p.116 C3

Vegetarians should head straight for this rare oasis in a corner of the city that seems to be trying hard to oust the meat-eaters with equally vegetarian Parsifal just across the road. A light, bright space, Zencefil even rises to its own delicious *limonata (*lemonade),

Left: in a city on the water, fresh fish is the thing to try.

Right: the wonderful view from Müzedechanga.

a traditional Turkish drink that has come roaring back into fashion.

NİŞANTAŞI, TEŞVİKİYE AND MAÇKA
Beymen Brasserie
Abdi İpekçi Caddesi 23/1, Nişantaşı; tel: 0212-343 0444; daily 10am–11pm; €€€; Metro: Osmanbey, then 15-minute walk

Rated the city's top pavement cafés by the Hürriyet newspaper, the Beymen Brasserie is a see-and-be-seen place par excellence where in summer you'll fight to find a seat at any of those much treasured pavement tables. The menu is French-influenced, with salad Niçoise one of the biggest sellers.

THE BOSPHORUS
Lavanta
Mecidiye Köprü Sokak 16, Ortaköy; tel: 0212-227 2995; www.lavantarestaurant.com; daily noon–midnight; €€€€; bus: 25RE from Kabataş

Housed in a rambling old house just steps from the water in fashionable Ortaköy, Lavanta is the İstanbul incarnation of a restaurant that started life in uber-fashionable Alaçatı, near Çeşme. One of its biggest assets is that the variety of rooms spread out over the floors ensures that groups of all sizes can eat in privacy. The menu is international, the quality of the cooking superb.

Lucca
Cevdetpaşa Caddesi 51/B, Bebek; tel: 0212-257 1255; daily 10am–2am; €€€€; bus: 25RE from Kabataş

Next to the Beyman

> İstanbul is slowly surrendering to the chain restaurants. Luckily the chains are often Turkish owned and offer a reliable and high-quality dining experience. Names to conjure with include The House Café which offers a fusion menu of falafels and kebabs in very attractive settings; Midpoint which boasts a lengthy menu of comfort foods such as pastas and quesadillas; and Kitchenette which doubles as a café and restaurant.

Brasserie this must surely be the city's second most popular place for people to lurk on the pavement and watch what's going on while chowing down on a not especially imaginative menu of international favourites. It's a younger, edgier crowd than at Beymen's, hence the DJ who rocks up in early evening to entertain the diners.

Müzedechanga
Sakıp Sabancı Museum; Sakıp Sabancı Caddesi 22, Emirgan; tel: 0212-323 0901; www.changa-İstanbul.com; Tue–Sun 10am–1am; €€€€; bus: 25RE from Kabataş

Views don't get much more spectacular than from the deck of the Müzedechanga where a wonderful menu of

originals such as soft goat's cheese on *katmer* (imagine the Indian *paratha*-like bread) are dished up with the utmost attention to good service.

KADIKÖY AND ÜSKÜDAR
Çiya
Caferağa Mahallesi, Güneşlibahçe Sokak 44, Kadıköy; tel: 0216-418 5115; daily 11.30am–10pm; €€€; ferry: Kadıköy, then 10-minute walk

This is one of İstanbul's great foodies treats. Çiya is a gourmet heaven spread over three buildings facing each other across the street, Çiya's food has become so famous that the restaurant even has its own magazine. Drawing much of its inspiration from the area around Gaziantep in the southeast, the menu features all sorts of dishes that can't be found elsewhere.

> Price per person for a single meze platter and/or soup, a main course, and one drink, in euros:
> €= under €10
> €€ = €10-18
> €€€ = €18-25
> €€€€ = over €25

103

Sport

İstanbul is a city of football lovers. One of the best ways to endear yourself is to start up a conversation about one of the three major city soccer teams, Galatasaray, Fenerbahçe and Beşiktaş. The big international spectator sport of the year is Formula One which takes place on a specially designed circuit out of town at Tuzla. There is also a horse-racing stadium at Bakırköy. For those who prefer to take part rather than just watch there are swimming pools in several of the larger hotels, and golf facilities way out at Kemerburgaz. Every year the Avrasya Marathon brings traffic on the Bosphorus Bridge to a halt.

> Every July a trans-continental swimming race takes place on the Bosphorus. For dates and details go to www.bosphorus.com.

FOOTBALL

KARAKÖY, TOPHANE AND BEŞIKTAŞ

Beşiktaş
İnönü Stadium, Süleyman Seba Caddesi, Beşiktaş; tel: 0212-310 1000; www.bjk.com.tr; charge; tram: Kabataş; map p.117 D4
Nicknamed the Black Eagles, Beşiktaş play, in a black and white strip, in a stadium that is very easy for visitors to get to. An unexpected extra is that you get to gaze out over the Bosphorus should the excitement of the game itself ever pall.

KADIKÖY AND ÜSKÜDAR

Fenerbahçe
Rüştü Saraçoğlu Stadium, Kadıköy; tel: 0216-542 1907; www.fenerbahce.org.tr; charge; ferry: Kadıköy, then 20-minute walk

Nicknamed the Yellow Canaries, Fenerbahçe play, in a yellow and navy strip, in another stadium that is relatively easy for non-car-owning visitors to get to.

GREATER İSTANBUL

Galatasaray
Türk Telekom Arena, Aslantepe; www.galatasaray.org; charge; private transport needed
Nicknamed Cim Bon or the Lions, Galatasaray may be the best known of all Turkey's football teams outside the country but neither their old stadium at

---

Below: golf is increasingly popular in Turkey.

Mecidiyeköy or their new one at Aslantepe is especially easy to get to from the main tourist areas. Playing in red and yellow, Galatasaray have been the most successful of all Turkish teams, winning both the UEFA Cup and Super Cup.

FORMULA ONE RACING

GREATER İSTANBUL

İstanbul Park
Göçbeyli Köyü Yolu; Tuzla; tel: 0216-556 9800; www.İstanbul parkcurcuit.com; charge; shuttle bus: from İstanbul airport, Taksim Square, Sultanahmet and elsewhere
İstanbul hosts Formula One racing at the end of May (although the date has changed frequently). The purpose-designed circuit is regarded as very challenging with 14 sharp bends (Turn Eight is seen as especially tough) laid out anti-clockwise with a gradient variant of 46 metres and several stretches which allow for speeds of up to 330km/hr.

Left: Beşiktaş football club's stadium is easy to reach.

On the third Sunday in October every year the Avrasya (Eurasia) Marathon (www.stanbulmarathon.org) is run from the Asian side of the Bosphorus Bridge across to the European side and then on to the Hippodrome.

tel: 0212-326 4646; www.kempinski-İstanbul.com; daily 7am–7pm May–Oct; charge; bus: 25RE from Kabataş
After a swim at this hotel pool few will ever seem as luxurious or have such a view as this glorious infinity version that seems to spill straight out into the Bosphorus.

GOLF

GREATER İSTANBUL

Kemer Golf and Country Club
Kemerburgaz; tel: 0212-239 7010; www.kemercountry.com; charge; private transport needed
On the edge of the Belgrade Forest, the Kemer Golf Club has an 18-hole championship green in a lovely, forested setting. It's open to men and women.

HORSE RACING

GREATER İSTANBUL

Veliefendi Hippodrome
Ekrem Kurt Bulvarı, Bakırköy; tel: 0212-444 0855; www.tjk.org; charge; train: Bakırköy
The last Sunday of June sees this hundred-year-old hippodrome with its 2,400-metre track staging its biggest event of the year, the Gazi Derby, named in honour of Mustafa Kemal Atatürk. There are also races here throughout the year but this is by far the most popular day out.

SWIMMING

Although you will see young men jumping into the Bosphorus on hot summer days you'd be ill-advised to join them. For a wild swim you're best off heading north to Kilyos *(see p.97)*, but there are several hotels with outdoor swimming pools that are open to non-guests, albeit at steep prices.

KARAKÖY, TOPHANE AND BEŞİKTAŞ

Cırağan Palace Kempinski Hotel
Çırağan Caddesi 32, Beşiktaş;

NİŞANTAŞI, TEŞVİKİYE AND MAÇKA

Hilton Hotel
Cumhuriyet Caddesi; tel: 0212-315 6000; www.İstanbul.hilton.com; daily 8am–8pm May–Oct; charge; funicular: Taksim, then taxi
The Hilton has the considerable asset that it was established before the city became so built up which means that it has extensive grounds with plenty of space for a pool and plenty of sun loungers.

Below: the annual Formula One race is a major event.

Transport

Depending on where you're coming from İstanbul's transport system will seem either wonderful (the US) or chaotic (Germany), but even its detractors concede that vast sums of money have been invested in infrastructure over the last decade with yet more spending to come. But İstanbul is an old city whose narrow streets were never designed for the pressure now put on them and during rush hour, especially in winter, traffic crawls through the streets. The coast road from Beşiktaş to Kuruçeşme is a bottleneck especially at weekends; the two Bosphorus bridges are similarly prone to snarl ups.

The local airline Turkish Airlines (THY) has a good safety and punctuality record on international flights and service is usually reasonably good, as is the food (always halal). The air travel high season is usually late December to mid-January, mid-March to mid-April and mid-June to mid-September.

GETTING THERE

BY SEA

It's only possible to get to İstanbul by ship if you are on a cruise. Cruise ships currently dock at the Karaköy International Maritime Passenger Terminal (tel: 0212-249 5576; tram: Karaköy; map p.116 B1), a short walk from the Galata Bridge, although there are mooted plans for a new Galataport at Tophane.

BY ROAD

Few people would want to embark on the three-day marathon that would be a journey by bus from northern Europe to İstanbul. However, there are daily buses from Sofia in Bul-garia and Bucharest in Romania as well as several a week from Athens in Greece. All will bring you to the Esenler bus station in İstanbul (Esenler Otogarı, Bayrampaşa; tel: 0212-658 0505; www.otogarİstanbul.com; tram: Otogar).

Entry Regulations

Driving to İstanbul is not a problem with few border formalities unless you want to import your car for more than six months. You can enter the country by road from Greece or Bulgaria.

BY TRAIN

You can get to İstanbul on the Bosphorus Express (Bosfor Ekspresi) train from Budapest in Hungary, Bucharest in Romania and Sofia in Bulgaria although you should not expect a speedy or luxurious journey – there's no buffet car, for example. Trains arrive at Sirkeci Station (Ankara Caddesi, Sirkeci; tel: 0212-527 0051; tram: Sirkeci; map p.121 D3) which was originally built for the late lamented

Below: the majority of visitors arrive by air.

Airports

Like many capital cities, İstanbul has two international airports: Atatürk International Airport (Atatürk Havalimanı, Yeşilköy; tel: 0212-465 3000; www.ataturkairport. com; metro: Havalimanı) and Sabiha Gökçen (Sabiha Gökçen Uluslararası Havaalanı, Pendik; tel: 0216-585 5000; www.sgair port.com; Havaş airport bus or private transfer). Most scheduled flights use Atatürk International Airport which, fortunately, is better connected to public transport. Cheaper flights often use Sahiba Gökçen which involves a long and relatively expensive transfer to Sultanahmet or Beyoğlu.

Havaş (tel: 0212-444 0487; www.havas.net/en) provides reasonably-priced airport transfers from Taksim Square to Atatürk International Airport and Sabiha Gökçen. Those to Atatürk Airport run every 30 minutes or so, those to Sabiha Gökçen every hour.

GETTING AROUND

BUS

İstanbul has a superb bus network although it can be difficult for non-Turkish-speakers to navigate their way around it. For visitors probably the two most useful bus terminals are at Eminönü and Taksim Square whence buses fan out to most of the places they are likely to want to visit. It's also easy to pick up a bus at the Kabataş interchange with the tram from Sultanahmet to travel along the European shore of the Bosphorus. To travel along its Asian

Most locals own an Akbil, a gem of an electronic purse consisting of a plastic device with a metal tab on it that is pressed into a machine as you board any form of city transport so that the fare can be deducted. You pay an initial deposit to buy an Akbil and can then load it with however much money you want. When its runs out you reload at an Akbil Satış Noktası or via machines at main terminals. Unfortunately the authorities plan to phase out the marvelous Akbil in favour of an electronic card that will supposedly perform the same function.

although British passengers may want to look at easyJet (www.easyjet.com) which flies from Luton to the city's second airport, Sabiha Gökçen; you will need to decide whether the additional costs of getting to and from these two airports don't outweigh the saving on the actual flight. From the UK there are also sometimes bargain flights on the Turkish airline Pegasus (**www.flypgs.com. tr**). The cheapest flights from Europe to Turkey are usually from Germany.

Below: one of İstanbul's efficient trams.

Orient Express service from Paris.

BY AIR

Airlines
Most national airlines fly into İstanbul. Note there are no direct flights from Canada or New Zealand.

Air Fares
Air fares to İstanbul are usually reasonably priced outside high season,

shore you'll find buses lined up opposite the ferry terminal at Üsküdar.

Although you can still pay on a few buses, most require that you buy a ticket in advance from a booth near the bus stop. Where there is no ticket booth a local kiosk may sell tickets. Bus tickets cost a flat TL1.50.

DOLMUŞ

The original dolmuşes were large yellow taxis which squeezed in as many passengers as possible and dropped them off anywhere along their route. Today's dolmuşes are merely minibuses that ply set routes in competition with or as additions to the bus services. Fares, paid direct to the driver, are the same or slightly higher than on buses. Visitors are unlikely to use many dolmuşes although there is a handy route from Beşiktaş (near the footbridge) to Taksim, and another that runs from beside the Naval Museum in Beşiktaş to the Military Museum in Harbiye.

FERRY

Escape the heat and traffic congestion by using one of the many ferries operated by İstanbul Deniz Otobüsleri (İDO; tel: 0212-444 4436; www.ido.com.tr). At Eminönü there are four prominent jetties (*iskele*)

serving the Harem bus terminal, Kadıköy, Üsküdar and the Bosphorus as well as a less obvious one serving the Golden Horn in front of the Zindan building housing the Storks nightclub. At Karaköy there is a terminal serving Haydarpaşa train station and Kadıköy, while at Kabataş there's a terminal serving the Princes' Islands. There are also intermittent ferry services between some of the Bosphorus suburbs. Full timetables are available at all the terminals.

FUNICULAR AND CABLE CAR

İstanbul has two important funiculars that link İstiklal Caddesi in Beyoğlu with the tram line. The first, between Karaköy and Tünel, has been in business for over a hundred years; the second, between Kabataş and Taksim, only came into service in 2006 but transformed the way in which people could move around the city.

The city also has two cable cars, one carrying passengers up from Eyüp waterfront to the Pierre Loti Café, the other swing-

Above: cable cars provide unbeatable views.

ing across Demokrasi Park from Maçka to Elmadağ, near Taksim.

METRO

İstanbul has two Metro lines, the first and most useful to visitors running from Aksaray to the airport (Havalimanı) via the bus station (Otogar), the second running from Taksim to 4.Levent. The Metro connects with the tram line via a short walk involving a bridge and underpass at Aksaray and directly at Zeytinburnu.

METROBUS

In 2009 a Metrobus service joined the other ways of getting around the city and was so successful

Below: ferries run between the European and Asian shores.

Carbon calculators such as CarbonOrg (www.climatecare. org) allow air travellers to offset their carbon footprint with a financial contribution to sustainable schemes worldwide that aim to reduce the effects of global warming.

The Marmaray is a multi-million-dollar Japanese-backed project to ease traffic congestion by building a tunnel under the Bosphorus from Sarayburnu to Üsküdar. When completed it will connect with the local (banliyö) trains that run from Sirkeci and Haydarpaşa, making it much easier to move around the city. The original completion date of 2010 had to be put back when excavation for a new station at Yenikapı uncovered the medieval port. It should now be completed by 2012 whereupon the historic stations at Sirkeci and Haydarpaşa will be decommissioned.

Above: it is easy to spot the bright yellow taxis.

that almost all the very regular services were immediately jam-packed. For short-term visitors, however, the Metrobus is of limited use since it mainly runs to the suburbs.

TAXIS

The city is served by a fleet of thousands of bright yellow taxis that are obliged by law to run their meters. Most taxi drivers are pleasant and helpful although some drive like lunatics and others take their passengers for the wrong sort of ride. The soaring price of petrol has pushed up taxi fares recently, and you should expect to pay around TL30 for a journey from the airport to Sultanahmet, and around TL10 from Sultanahmet to Taksim.

TRAIN

A dreadfully battered suburban train service operates from Sirkeci to Halkali passing through Cankurtaran for Sultanahmet. Visitors might want to use it to get to Kumkapı or Yedikule. On the Asian side of the city a similar service from Haydarpaşa to Gebze is of little interest to visitors.

TRAM

The tram (called *tramway* in Turkish) is an indispensible asset for visitors since it runs along Divan Yolu connecting Sultanahmet to the Grand Bazaar, as well as running downhill from Sultanahmet to the ferry terminals at Eminönü and then across the Galata Bridge to the terminal at Kabataş where there's a direct connection with the funicular to Taksim. Services are frequent although they stop at midnight, and carriages are air-conditioned.

There is also a nostalgic tram that runs from Taksim Square along İstiklal Caddesi to Tünel. It makes for a fun ride although it's slow and only runs three or four times an hour.

DRIVING

Driving a car in İstanbul is for masochists only. Not only is the traffic conges-tion terrible and parking a headache but car hire is also expensive and Turkish petrol prices said to be the highest in the world. Do us all a favour and stick with public transport but if you absolutely must use a car the website of the Turkish Automobile Association has all the details (Türkiye Turing ve Otomobil Kurumu; Sanayi Sitesi Yanı 4, Levent; tel: 0212-282 8140, www.turing.org.tr).

CAR HIRE FIRMS

Avis
Atatürk International Airport; tel: 0212-465 3455; www.avis.com.tr; Sabiha Gökçen Airport; tel: 0216-585 5154

Hertz
Atatürk International Airport; tel: 0212-465 5999; www.hertz.com.tr; Sabiha Gökçen Airport; tel: 0216-588 0141

Recently İstanbul sprouted a fleet of water taxis (Deniztaksi; tel: 0212-444 4436; www.deniztaksi.com.tr) that can be called to order just like normal taxis. At the moment they are only suitable for groups but if the experiment works out they may become more widely useful.

Walks and Views

In a city dominated by water, the most prized asset a hotel or restaurant can claim is a view, be it of the Sea of Marmara, the Bosphorus or the Golden Horn. Nothing can be more enthralling than to gaze out over the domes and minarets peeking up from the greenery beyond Sarayburnu, or to let your eye linger on the bumps of the Princes' Islands emerging from the mist. On a hot summer's day it's easier to sit in a café and admire the view than to set off on a walk. Still, there are some great strolls that don't demand too much energy, as well as a longer one along the city walls best kept for cooler days.

VIEWS

SULTANAHMET AND KUMKAPI

Setüstü Çay Bahçesi
Gülhane Park, Sultanahmet; tram: Gülhane; map p.121 D3
A row of alluring tea gardens inside Gülhane Park are lined up to scoop the view of the confluence of the Sea of Marmara, the Bosphorus and the Golden Horn. The tea is served in samovars here so bring along some friends to share.

SEE ALSO:
Doydoy Restaurant (p.98)
Fourth courtyard of Topkapı Palace (p.93)
Mavi Ev Hotel (p.61)
Sarı Konak Hotel (p.62)

BEYAZIT AND FATİH

Büyük Valide Han
Çakmakçılar Yokusu, Tahtakale; tram: Beyazıt, then 15-minute walk; map p.120 C3
If you can find the man with the key to take you onto the roof of this *han* the view all the way back down the Golden Horn and

Above: enjoying the view from Pierre Loti Café.

up the Bosphorus to the first bridge is nothing short of breathtaking.

SEE ALSO:
Botanical Garden (p.97)

EMİNÖNÜ AND THE GOLDEN HORN

Pierre Loti Café (p.29)

KARAKÖY, TOPHANE AND BEŞİKTAŞ

Çırağan Palace Kempinski Hotel (p.63)
Four Seasons İstanbul at the Bosphorus (p.63)
İstanbul Modern Café (p.101)

BEYOĞLU

Cihangir Mosque
Cihangir Yokuşu, Cihangir; tram: Kabataş, then 15-minute uphill walk; map p.117 C2
It's not the mosque that matters (although it's very pretty). Instead behind it are a couple of benches poised to soak up a peerless Bosphorus view.

SEE ALSO:
360 (p.101)
Galata Tower (p.76)
Leb-i Derya (p.102)
Mikla (p.102)
The Marmara (p.66)

THE BOSPHORUS

Aşiyan
Bebek-Rumeli Hisarı Caddesi, Rumeli Hisarı; Tue–Sat 9am–5pm; free; bus: 25RE from Kabataş
One-time home and burial place of the poet Tevfik Fikret (1867–1915), Aşiyan boasts one of the finest views in the city from its upstairs windows.

SEE ALSO:
Beylerbeyi Palace (p.95)
Kücüksu Kasrı (p.95)

Left: looking out over the mighty Bosphorus.

(Bebek Park; tel: 0212-257 6651; daily 8am–11pm) or Sade Kahve (Bebek-Rumeli Hisarı Caddesi; tel: 0212-358 2324; daily 8am–10pm). Bus No. 25RE from Kabataş stops in both suburbs.

GREATER İSTANBUL

Yedikule to Ayvansaray

It is best not to walk the length of the land walls alone as they can be home to unsavoury characters. Take the suburban train from Cankurtaran to Yedikule and head north. At Topkapı you can divert to the Panorama 1453 Museum. North of Topkapı the Tekfur Sarayı was an imperial palace. Beyond are two towers and then you reach the Golden Horn at Ayvansaray where bus No. 99A will run you back to Eminönü. The whole walk takes around six hours to complete.

ORGANISED WALKS

Urban Adventures

Intrepid Travel, Ticarethane Sokak 11/1, Sultanahmet; www.urbanadventures.com; Mon-Sat 9am-5pm; tram: Sultanahmet; map p.121 D2

Below: the impressive Firuz Ağa Mosque.

Müzedechanga *(p.103)*
Rumeli Hisarı Castle *(p.77)*

KADIKÖY AND ÜSKÜDAR

Büyük Çamlıca

Turistik Çamlıca Caddesi, Üsküdar; free; bus: from Üsküdar

The highest point in İstanbul, Büyük Çamlıca (288 metres) was always feted for its spectacular views along the Bosphorus. Today the views are a little spoilt by telephone masts but it's a great place for a picnic or a quick drink at the Ottoman-themed café.

GREATER İSTANBUL

St George's Monastery

Büyükada; tel: 0216-382 1333; Apr–Sep daily 10am–6pm, Oct–Mar Sat–Sun 10am–5pm; ferry: Büyükada

Scene of an annual pilgrimage every 23 April, St George's Monastery on Büyükada is home to the Yücetepe Kır Gazinosu, a simple meatballs-and-chips venue that boasts a truly spectacular view.
SEE ALSO FESTIVALS, P.48

Some stretches of the shore of the Golden Horn have recently been landscaped with walkways. There's a particularly pleasant waterside stroll from Unkapanı by the Atatürk Bridge to Ayvansaray.

WALKS

SULTANAHMET AND KUMKAPI

Sultanahmet to Çemberlitaş

Start in front of the Milion opposite Sultanahmet Square and head west along Divan Yolu. On the way you'll pass the Firuz Ağa Mosque, an imperial mausoleum, and the 17th-century Köprülü Library. The tram stops at Sultanahmet and Çemberlitaş make convenient start and end points.

THE BOSPHORUS

Bebek to Rumeli Hisarı

A half-hour stroll along the promenade linking the two suburbs. You can stop for a drink afterwards at either the Boğaziçi Bebek Café

Atlas

The following streetplan of İstanbul makes it easy to find the attractions listed in the A–Z section. A selective index to streets and sights will help you find other locations throughout the city

Map Legend

Freeway			Metro station
Divided highway			Tourist information
Main roads		★	Sight of interest
Minor roads			Museum or gallery
Ferry			Mosque
Tram line / station			Cathedral or church
Railroad			Synagogue
Funicular rail			Bus station
Cable car			Main post office
Pedestrian area			Tower
Notable building			Theatre
Park		†	Monastery
Urban area			Viewpoint
Non urban area		✈	Airport

p114	p115	p116	p117
p118	p119	p120	p121

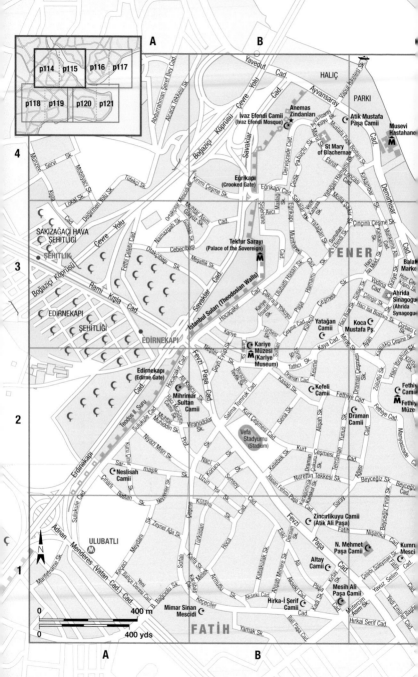

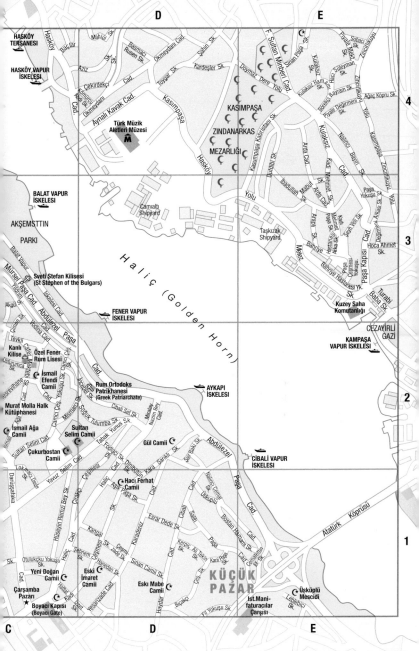

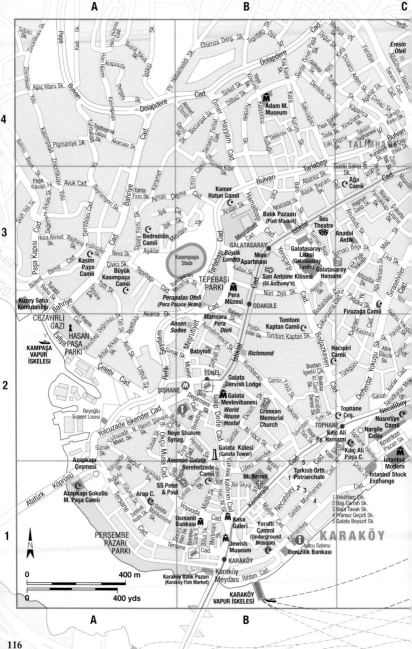

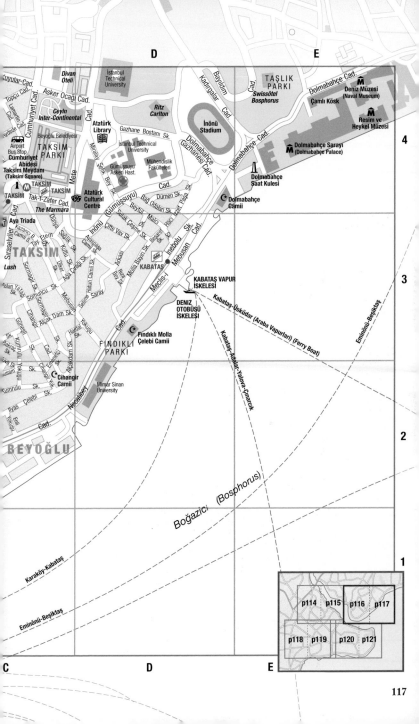

D

E

Kuyular-Cad.

Topçu Cad.

Cumhuriyet Cad.

Divan Oteli

Asker Ocağı Cad.

İstanbul Technical University

TAŞLIK PARKI

Dolmabahçe Cad.

Deniz Müzesi (Naval Museum)

Ritz Carlton

Swissôtel Bosphorus

Çamlı Köşk

Ceylin Inter-Continental

Beyoğlu Belediyesi

Gazhane Bostanı Sk.

Resim ve Heykel Müzesi

Airport Bus Stop

Atatürk Library

TAKSİM PARKI

İstanbul Technical University

İnönü Stadium

Gümüşsuyu Askeri Hast.

Mühendislik Fakülteleri

Dolmabahçe Sarayı (Dolmabahçe Palace)

Cumhuriyet Abidesi

Taksim Meydanı (Taksim Square)

4

Miralay Şefik Bey Sk.

Meta

Dolmabahçe Saat Kulesi

TAKSİM

Tak-î-Zafer Cad.

TAKSİM

İnönü (Gümüşsuyu) Cad.

Dümen Sk.

Bağ Odaları Sk.

İzzet Paşa Sk.

TAKSİM

Atatürk Cultural Centre

The Marmara

Aya Triada

Kazancı B.

Kazancı Camii Sk.

Tav Sk.

Etem

Sıraselviler Cad.

Dolmabahçe Camii

Çifte Yav Sk.

Malçı

Hacı

Sıdık Çeşme Sk.

Beytül

Bezergi Sk.

Mebusan

Lush

Dünya Sk.

Sıdık Sk.

Anbarlı

Camii Sk.

İlker Sk.

Ağa Çeşli Sk.

Aslan Yatağı Sk.

Sümbül Sk.

Somuncu Sk.

Alçak Dam. Sk.

Hantal Sk.

KABATAŞ

Reşa

Molla Bayırı Sk.

Selime Hatun Camii Sk.

Saray

3

Sormagit Sk.

Güneşli

Cihangir Sk.

Yokuşu

Cihangir

KABATAŞ VAPUR İSKELESİ

Medis-i

Kabataş-Üsküdar (Araba Vapurları) (Ferry Boat)

Eminönü-Beşiktaş

Bakraç

Kumrulu Yokuşu

Bakraç Sk.

Susam

Kumrulu

FINDIKLI PARKI

Ağaçdam Sk.

Cihangir Sk.

DENİZ OTOBÜSÜ İSKELESİ

Fındıklı Molla Çelebi Camii

Kabataş-Adalar-Yalova-Çınarcık

İlyas Sk.

Çelebi Sk.

Emir Yokuşu

Cihangir Camii

Necatibey Cad.

Mimar Sinan University

Cad.

2

BEYOĞLU

Boğaziçi (Bosphorus)

1

Karaköy-Kabataş

Eminönü-Beşiktaş

| p114 | p115 | p116 | p117 |

| p118 | p119 | p120 | p121 |

C

D

E

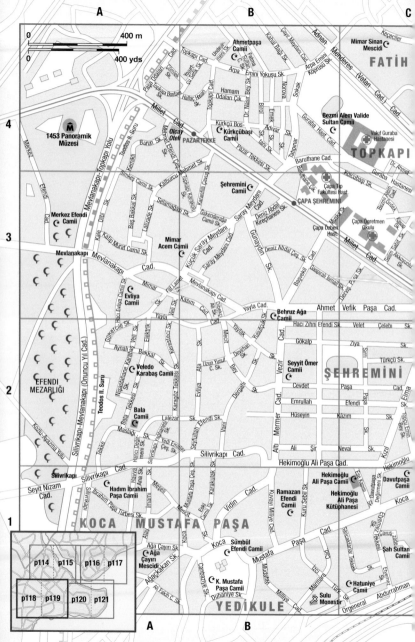

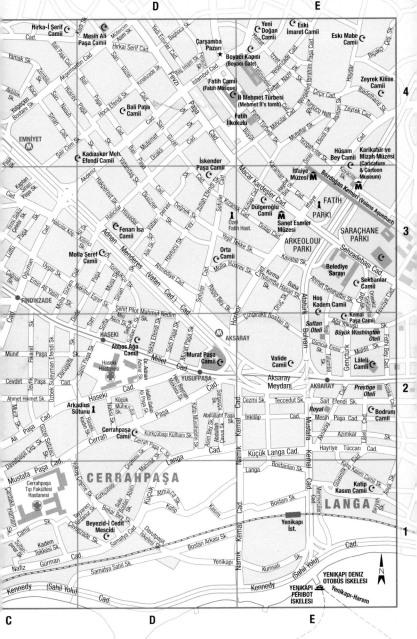

Map labels (by region):

Column D (top):
Hirka-I Şerif Camii
Mesih Ali Paşa Camii
Müteferm Paşa Camii
Çarşamba Pazarı
★ Boyacı Kapısı (Boyacı Gate)
Fatih Camii (Fatih Mosque)
II Mehmet Türbesi (Mehmet II's tomb)
Fatih İlkokulu

Column E (top):
Yeni Doğan Camii
Eski İmaret Camii
Eski Mabe Camii
Zeyrek Kilise Camii
İbadethane Sk.

Yamak Sk.
Akbiyık
Kaşan Sinan Paşa Cad.
EMNİYET Ⓜ
Kadıasker Meh. Efendi Camii
İskender Paşa Camii
Hüsam Bey Camii
Karikatür ve Mizah Müzesi (Caricature & Cartoon Museum)

Macar Kardeşler Cad.
İtfaiye Müzesi Ⓜ
Bozdoğan Kemeri (Valens Aqueduct)
FATİH PARKI

FINDIKZADE ●
Molla Şeref Camii
Fenari İsa Camii
Adnan Menderes (Vatan Cad.)
Dülgeroğlu Camii
Sanet Eserler Müzesi
Özel Fatih Hast.
Orta Camii
ARKEOLOUI PARKI
SARAÇHANE PARKI
Belediye Sarayı
Sekbanlar Camii
Şehzadebaşı Cad.

Şehit Pilot Mahmut Nedim Sk.
HASEKI
Abbas Ağa Camii
Haseki Hastanesi
Murat Paşa Camii
Ⓜ AKSARAY
Hoş Kadem Camii
Kemal Paşa Camii
Sultan Oteli
Büyük Washington Oteli
Valide Camii
Läleli Camii
Gençtürk

FINDIKZADE
Münif
Cevdet
Ahmet Hikmet Sk.
YUSUFPAŞA
Arkadius Sütunu ▲
Cerrahpaşa Camii
Aksaray Meydanı
AKSARAY ●
Prestige Oteli
Royal
Bodrum Camii
Mesih Paşa Cad.

Mustafa Paşa Cad.
Cerrahpaşa Tıp Fakültesi Hastanesi
CERRAHPAŞA
Küçük Langa Cad.
Katip Kasım Camii
LANGA

Beyezid-I Cedit Mescidi
Kadem Tekkesi Cad.
Yenikapı İst.
Kennedy (Sahil Yolu)

YENİKAPI DENİZ OTOBÜS İSKELESİ
YENİKAPI FERİBOT İSKELESİ
Yenikapı-Harem
N

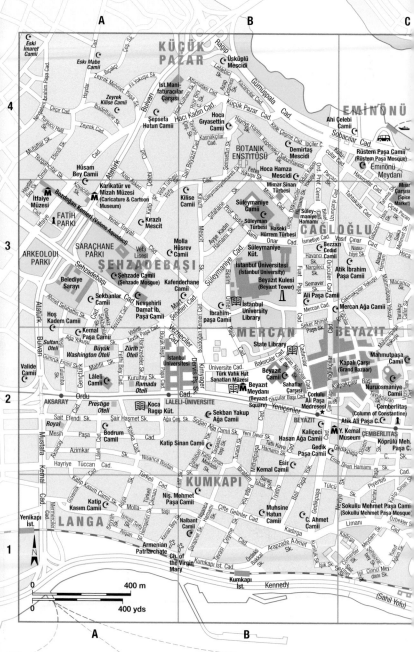

KARAKÖY

KARAKÖY Meydanı

Karaköy Balık Pazarı (Karaköy Fish Market)

KARAKÖY VAPUR İSKELESİ

Galata Köprüsü (Galata Bridge)

Rıhtım Cad.

Karaköy-Kabataş

Eminönü-Beşiktaş

Karaköy-Haydarpaşa-Kadıköy

Boğaziçi (Bosphorus)

Karaköy-Bakırköy

Sirkeci-Hârem (Araba Vapurları) (Ferry Boat)

İstanbul-Marmara-Akdeniz Hattı

ŞEHİRHATTI İSKELESİ

EMİNÖNÜ İSKELESİ

EMİNÖNÜ

SİRKECİ FERİBOT İSKELESİ

Reşadiye Cad.

SİRKECİ İSKELESİ

SARAY BURNU

Atatürk Heykeli

Yeni Camii (New Mosque)

Hatice Sultan Türbesi

Arpacılar Camii

Yalı Köşkü Cad.

Kennedy Cad.

Sirkeci İstasyon Cad.

Sirkeci İstasyonu (Sirkeci Railway Station)

Daye Hatun Mescidi

Goths Column

Babıâli Cad.

S. Hamit Türbesi

Hamidiye Cad.

Mimar Kemalettin Cad.

SİRKECİ

Ankara Cad.

İstasyon Arkası Sk.

Şehin Şah Pehlevi Cad.

Aşirefendi Cad.

İbni Kemal Cad.

Nöbethane Cad.

Hocapaşa Hamamı Sk.

Asir Ef. Sk.

GÜLHANE PARKI

Topkapı Sarayı (Topkapı Palace)

Hamdi Cemal Sk.

Nadir Sk.

Ebussuut Cad.

Karaki Hüs. Çelebi Camii

History of Islamic Science & Technology

Celal Ferdi Gökçay Sk.

Bâb-ı Âli Camii

İstanbul Vilayet

GÜLHANE

Arkeoloji Müzesi (Archaeology Museum)

Bab-ı Selam (Gate of Salutations)

Ankara Cad.

Bâb-ı Âli

Alemdar Cad.

Hükümet Konağı Sk.

Çağaloğlu Hamamı

Zeynep Sultan C.

Alay Köşkü

Çizme Kapısı (Cizme Gate)

Ticket Office

Şerefefendi Sk.

Nuruosmaniye Cad.

Ağa Camii

Prof. K. İsmail Gürkan Cad.

Türbedar Sk.

Babıâli Cad.

Molla Fenari Camii

Yerebatan Camii

Ayasofya Meydanı

Ayasofya Saraçları

Aya İrini (Church of St Eirene)

Alay Meydanı (First Court)

Çemberlitaş Hamamı

Çatal Sk.

Sağlık Mus.

Yerebatan Cad.

Yücelt Youth Hostel

Hotel Kybele

Yerebatan Sarnıcı (Basilica Cistern)

Cağaloğlu Sk.

Caferiye Sk.

Soğukçeşme Sk.

Aya Sofya (Church Holy Wisdom)

Bâb-ı Hümâyûn (Imperial Gate)

Sultan Ahmet III Çeşmesi (Fountain of Ahmet III)

Köprülü Küt.

Divan Yolu Cad.

Milion Cad.

SULTANAHMET

Binbirdirek Sarnıcı

Klodfarer Cad.

Piyer Loti Cad.

SULTANAHMET PARKI

Ayasofya Meydanı

Bâbıhümayun Cad.

İshak Paşa C.

Four Seasons Sultanahmet

Empress Zöe

Türk ve İslam Eserleri Müzesi (Museum of Turkish and Islamic Arts)

İbrahim Paşa

Hippodrome

Atmeydanı Sk.

Terzihane Cad.

Sultan Ahmet Türbesi

Haseki Hürrem Hamamı

Sultanahmet Sanatlar Çarşısı

Mimar Mehmet Ağa Cad.

Tevkifhane Sk.

Akbıyık Cad.

Mavi Ev

Magnaura Sarayı

Cankurtaran Tren Garı

Ahırkapı Feneri

Marmara Denizi (Sea of Marmara)

Şehit Mehm. Paşa Yokuşu Sk.

Sultan Ahmet Camii (Blue Mosque)

Tavukhane Sk.

Kabasakal Cad.

Kutlugün Sk.

Utangaç Sk.

Akbıyık Değirmeni Sk.

Hotel Poem

SULTANAHMET

Kasap Osman Sk.

Nakilbent Sk.

Kaleci Sk.

Küçük Ayasofya Cad.

Aksakal Sk.

Şifa Hamamı Sk.

Arasta Bazaar

Torun Sk.

Mozaik Müzesi

Nakilbent Camii

Küçük Ayasofya Camii

Avicenna

Cankurtaran Cad.

Ahırkapı Sk.

Oyuncu Sk.

Armada

Keresteci Hakkı Sk.

Şadırvan

Cad.

p114 p115 p116 p117

p118 p119 p120 p121

121

122

Index

Hotels

Restaurants

Cafes and Bars

Shops

Insight Smart Guide: İstanbul

Compiled by: Pat Yale
Commissioned by: Sarah Sweeney
Edited by: Maria Lord
Proofread by: Leonie Wilding
Indexed by: Michael Macaroon

All pictures APA/Rebecca Erol except: Courtesy Admar Hotel; Kim Ahistrom 89; Alamy 17L; Vycheslav Argenberg 7B; Ayhang 105T; Henri Bergius 19B, 97; Captain orange 30T; Scot Dexter 90; Dysturb.net 37T; Rebecca Erol 11, 13, 23T, 42, 49T, 95T, 97T; Getty Images 23; Greenwich Photolibrary 16; Courtesy Hotel Ibrahim Pasha; Istockphoto 12, 44, 45, 95; Isa Kocher 48; Jerzy Kociatkiewicz 55; Herry Prasad Kholkute 91T; Lawford 62; Josiah Mackensie 65; Marmaduk 30; Aaron May 98; Monkey Mishkin 54; Procsilas Moscas 57; One2c 6, 21, 31; Alara Orhon 105; Photolibrary.com 111; John Picken 100; Charles Remenak 17R; Dick Rochester 106; Turkish Culture and Tourism 3BL, 32, 49, 50, 71, 73T, 79, 80, 103, 104, 112/113; Simonetta Viterbi 47; Vladimir Shioshvilli 99; William White 110
Cover picture by: Photolibrary.com

Picture Manager: Steven Lawrence

Maps: Phoenix Mapping and James Macdonald
Series Editor: Sarah Sweeney

First Edition 2011
© 2011 Apa Publications GmbH & Co.
Verlag KG Singapore Branch, Singapore.

Printed by CTPS-China

Worldwide distribution enquiries:
APA Publications GmbH & Co Verlag KG
(Singapore branch)
7030 Ang Mo Kio Ave 5
08-65 Northstar @ AMK
Singapore 569880
email: apasin@signet.com.sg

Distributed in the UK and Ireland by:
GeoCenter International Ltd
Meridian House,
Churchill Way West,
Basingstoke,
Hampshire, RG21 6YR;
tel: (44 1256) 817 987;
email: sales@geocenter.co.uk

Distributed in the United States by:
Ingram Publisher Services
One Ingram Blvd, PO Box 3006
La Vergne, TN 37086-1986
email: customer.service@ingrampublisher services.com

Distributed in Australia by:
Universal Publishers,
1 Waterloo Road,
Macquarie Park, NSW 2113;
tel: (61) 2-9857 3700;
email: sales@universalpublishers.com.au

Distributed in New Zealand by:
Hema Maps New Zealand Ltd (HNZ),
Unit 2, 10 Cryers Road,
East Tamaki, Auckland 2013;
tel: (64) 9-273 6459;
email: sales.hema@clear.net.nz

Contacting the Editors
We would appreciate it if readers would alert us to errors or outdated information by writing to:
Apa Publications, PO Box 7910, London SE1 1WE, UK; fax: (44 20) 7403 0290; email: insight@apaguide.co.uk

No part of this book may be reproduced, stored in a retrieval system or transmitted in any form or by any means (electronic, mechanical, photocopying, recording or otherwise), without prior written permission of Apa Publications. Brief text quotations with use of photographs are exempted for book review purposes only. Information has been obtained from sources believed to be reliable, but its accuracy and completeness, and the opinions based thereon, are not guaranteed.

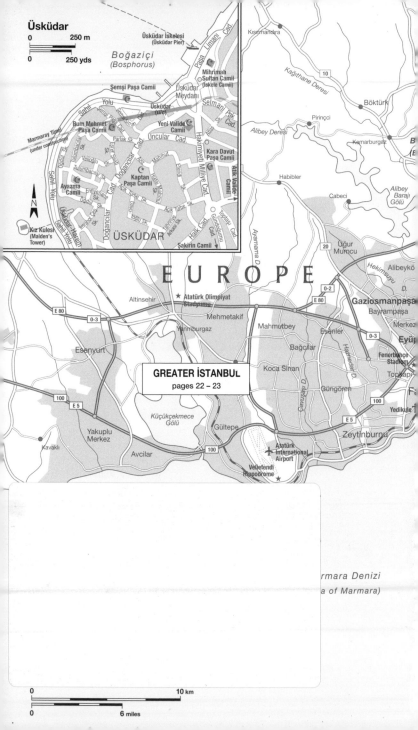

Üsküdar

0 — 250 m
0 — 250 yds

Boğaziçi
(Bosphorus)

Üsküdar İskelesi
(Üsküdar Pier)

Paşa Limanı Cad.

Kısımandıra

Mihrimah
Sultan Camii
(İskele Camii)

Şemşi Paşa Camii

Üsküdar
Meydanı

Selman Pak Cad.

Böktürk

10

Kağıthane Deresi

Üsküdar
(u/c)

Sahil
Yolu

Şemşi Paşa Sk.

Şerefiye Sk.

Rum Mehmet
Paşa Camii

Yeni Valide
Camii

Uncular Cad.

Pirinççi

Alibey Deresi

Marmaray Tüneli
(under construction)

Parlak Sk.

Kemerburgaz

B
(E

Doğancılar Cad.

Hakimiyet

Tulumbacılar Sk.

Mahmut

Kara Davut
Paşa Camii

Atik Valide
Camii

Habibler

Velioğlu

Tulumbacılar Sk.

Elhuda

Milliye Cad.

Kaptan
Paşa Camii

Tavaşı

Alibeyköy

Alibey
Barajı
Gölü

Ayazma
Camii

Enfiyehane Cad.

Ödül Sk.

Doğancılar Cad.

Açık Türbe Sk.

Kışla Sk.

Tavaşi Mahmut

Cabeci

N

Üsküdar-Harem

Sahil Yolu

Kısla Sk.

Tabirhane Arkası Sk.

ÜSKÜDAR

Halk Cad.

Tenbel Hacı Mehmet Sk.

Toptaşı Cad.

Gündoğumu Cad.

Ayazma D.

Uğur
Mumcu

20

Hekimsuyu

D.

Kız Kulesi
(Maiden's
Tower)

Şakirin Camii

E U R O P E

0-2

Gaziosmanpaşa

E 80

Bayrampaşa

Merkez

Altınsehir

★ Atatürk Olimpiyat
Stadyumu

Mehmetakif

Mahmutbey

Esenler

0-3

Eyüp

E 80

0-3

Yanınburgaz

Bağcılar

Fenerbahce
Stadium

Esenyurt

Koca Sinan

Hazneden D.

Çavuşçay D.

Çarusçay D.

Topkapı

GREATER İSTANBUL
pages 22 – 23

Güngören

100

100

Yedikule

Küçükçekmece
Gölü

Gültepe

E 5

Zeytinburnu

Yakuplu
Merkez

E 5

100

Kavaklı

Avcılar

100

Atatürk
International
Airport

Veliefendi
Hippodrome ★

rmara Denizi
a of Marmara)

0 — 10 km
0 — 6 miles